DOG CARE
Companions™

The Secret Lives of Dogs

The Real Reasons behind 52 Mysterious Canine Behaviors

By Jana Murphy
and the Editors of

RODALE

Notice

This book is intended as a reference volume only, not as a medical manual. The information given here is designed to help you make informed decisions about your pet's behavior. It is not intended as a substitute for any treatment that may have been recommended by your veterinarian. If you suspect that your pet has a serious behavior problem, we urge you to seek competent help.

Library of Congress Cataloging-in-Publication Data

Murphy, Jana.
    The secret lives of dogs : the real reasons behind 52 mysterious canine behaviors / by Jana Murphy and the editors of Pets, part of the family.
        p.   cm. — (Dog care companions)
    Includes index.
    ISBN 1–57954–255–7 hardcover
    ISBN 1–57954–312–X paperback
    1. Dogs—Behavior.   2. Dogs—Training.   I. Pets, part of the family.   II. Series.
SF433 .M87   2000
636.7'0887—dc21   99–059184

Distributed to the book trade by St. Martin's Press

2 4 6 8 10 9 7 5 3   hardcover
    4 6 8 10 9 7 5 3   paperback

Visit us on the Web at www.petspartofthefamily.com, or call us toll-free at (800) 848-4735.

OUR PURPOSE

To explore, celebrate, and stand in awe before the special relationship between us and the animals who share our lives.

Pets
part of the family

The Secret
Lives of Dogs

The Secret Lives of Dogs

AUTHOR
Jana Murphy

RODALE ACTIVE LIVING BOOKS

Editor: Matthew Hoffman
Publisher: Neil Wertheimer
Editorial Director: Michael Ward
Research Manager: Ann Gossy Yermish
Copy Manager: Lisa D. Andruscavage
Copy Editors: Kathryn C. LeSage, Karen Neely
Cover Designer and Design Coordinator: Joanna Reinhart
Associate Studio Manager: Thomas P. Aczel
Book Manufacturing Director: Helen Clogston
Manufacturing Manager: Mark Krahforst

WELDON OWEN PTY LTD

Chairman: John Owen
Publisher: Sheena Coupe
Associate Publisher: Lynn Humphries
Senior Editor: Janine Flew
Senior Designer: Kylie Mulquin
Designer: Jacqueline Richards
Icons: Matt Graif, Chris Wilson/Merilake
Indexer: Barbara Long
Production Manager: Caroline Webber
Production Assistant: Kylie Lawson

Film separation by Colourscan Co. Pte. Ltd., Singapore

CONTENTS

PART ONE

"I'VE ALWAYS DONE IT THIS WAY"

Ancient Instincts and Urges

CONTENTS

PART FOUR
_____

"I Like the Good Things in Life"

The Passion for Food and Fun

PART FIVE

"MY BODY MAKES ME DO IT"

When Anatomy Is Destiny

Introduction

Dogs have been part of our families for so long that we often think of them as little (and not entirely well-behaved) humans. Sometimes, we forget that they're an entirely different species. They do things for reasons that have nothing to do with us—reasons that, in some cases, are millions of years old.

Last week, for example, I took Molly, my Labrador retriever, for a walk in the outdoor market near our home. On the sidewalk outside a pizza shop, she stopped to investigate a spot about the size of a pencil point. She gave it a sniff, then flopped on her back and vigorously rolled back and forth. Whatever the spot was, she was rubbing it as deeply into her coat as she possibly could.

Molly was obeying an ancient instinct. Dogs in the wild rolled on things to disguise their natural scents. Molly doesn't have to think about predators or prey, but those old memories still linger. Her rolling was a way of telling the world, "Ain't no one here but us pepperonis."

Dogs do a lot of things like this—things that, from a human point of view, don't make much sense. They bury bones. They walk past their water bowls to drink from the toilet. They chase their tails and steal each other's food. You've probably never been sure why they do the weird and wacky things that they do—until now.

The Secret Lives of Dogs explains the most common and most mysterious types of dog behavior. Take tail chasing. It looks like fun, but it's actually serious business. Dogs used to be hunters. Their eyes and brains are made in such a way that the slightest movement makes them think, "Rabbit!" Before they have a chance to think, "Hey, that's just my tail," their legs are already in motion—and around and around they go.

Dogs smell and hear things of which humans are totally unaware. This explains why many of the "odd" things that they do aren't so strange after all. Nearly every male dog, for example, will lift his leg on fire hydrants and sign poles. Why does he do it? Because he can smell every dog who's been there before, and he knows that future dogs will smell him. He wants them all to know how big and tough he is. Lifting his leg allows him to aim higher than the last guy.

This amazing sense of smell also explains why dogs put their noses in embarrassing places. They don't mean to be rude. They're just taking in loads of information: where you've been, who you've been around, and whether you're happy or sad—all from a quick sniff. A similar thing happens when they stick their heads out car windows, eat unpleasant things in the yard, or cock their heads when we talk. They're using their super-senses to catch up on what's happening around them.

Despite our many differences, dogs and humans get along very well. But occasionally, a dog's natural behavior causes trouble in the family. Destroying furniture. Drooling on the carpets. Biting when playing. Every chapter in *The Secret Lives of Dogs* is packed with practical tips for helping dogs behave better and enjoy life a little more. The "pepper solution" (it has to be red pepper) to dung eating. Why rawhides are better than rubber toys. How changing your posture can eliminate "submissive urination." Even ways to rub dogs' bellies and ears so they groan with pleasure.

Since dogs' breeds play a big role in how they act, we've also included a special feature called "Breed Specific." It explains why Labradors love to play with balls. Why Rottweilers lean on people. Why Akitas chase cats and German shepherds love tug-of-war. And dozens of other breed-specific habits.

To truly appreciate dogs, we have to understand how they think and what they see when they look at the world around them. *The Secret Lives of Dogs* is filled with insights into these wonderful animals. You'll understand them better, and at the same time, you'll discover hundreds of ways to make them happier in today's confusing world.

Matthew Hoffman

Matthew Hoffman
Editor, *Pets: Part of the Family* books

PART ONE

"I've Always Done It This Way"

Ancient Instincts and Urges

Although dogs have been living with people for a long time, some
of their behavior has its origins in their ancestors' days in the wild,
a time when dogs had to be totally self-sufficient in order to survive.

CHAPTER ONE

DISLIKE HAVING THEIR FEET TOUCHED

Memories of Pain

Dogs have very tough paw pads. The pads consist of tissue that's similar to callus, which can be as much as ³/₄-inch thick. It's as though dogs are walking on thick leather soles. They can walk comfortably on surfaces that would leave people wincing and hopping.

The rest of their feet, however, are a lot more sensitive—so much so that they hate having them touched. It seems to be a universal dislike. Regardless of the breed, most dogs will jerk away when you touch their feet, especially on top or between the toes.

This curious sensitivity wouldn't be a problem if it weren't for the fact that dogs periodically need to have their nails trimmed or their toes inspected for stones or burrs. Some dogs will put up with having their feet handled, but others will fight like crazy. It's not uncommon for groomers to charge an extra fee to provide what should be routine claw care.

Don't Mess with My Living

The bottoms of dogs' feet are designed to withstand rugged use, but the tops are not, says John C. Wright, Ph.D., a certified applied animal behaviorist; professor of psychology at Mercer University in Macon, Georgia; and author of *The Dog Who Would Be King*. The tops of the feet are loaded with nerve endings that fire off warnings when they sense pressure that could presage potential injuries, he explains. You can test this for yourself. Touch the bottom of your dog's feet, and he probably won't react. Touch the tops, and he'll pull away or flinch a little. Touch between his toes, and he'll make it clear that he'd really like to be left alone.

"Dogs' feet are essential for them to accomplish almost everything they do," explains

It's easiest to trim dogs' nails when they're on a high, slippery surface. They have to concentrate more on keeping their balance than on struggling with you.

Dr. Wright. "They're used in defense, for hunting, for locomotion, and even for communicating—dogs leave visual markers when they scratch the ground." So dogs get a little nervous when things (or people) that they can't control start touching their feet.

Remembering the Last Time

Dogs have thick, tough claws, and even routine pedicures can be uncomfortable—or worse. "A cut to the quick of the nail is very painful," says Lynn Cox, D.V.M., a veterinarian in Olive Branch, Mississippi. Dogs have good memories of things that have hurt them. The more they've been nicked by nail clippers, the more determined they'll be to keep their feet out of reach.

Bad memories may be compounded by the fact that some dogs only have their feet touched when they're being worked on. Neither nail trims nor first aid are experiences that dogs remember fondly. They come to believe that any foot contact is bad contact, and so they shy away from it.

Now That You Understand...

Lift them up to stop the fear. Dogs who are foot phobic at home sometimes get downright easy-natured when groomers or veterinarians lift their feet. It's not because experts have a magic touch. It's because they put dogs on

A FRIENDLY SHAKE

Shaking hands isn't merely a good social skill. Dogs who learn to shake hands get used to having their feet touched. They get a lot of compliments for their good manners. And they enjoy it so much, you may have trouble getting them to stop.

While your dog is sitting, reach your hand toward him, palm-up, at the usual shaking level. Most dogs will instinctively reach forward, although some won't get the idea unless you pick up the paw and give it a shake. In either case, say "shake" once you're holding the paw. Then praise him a lot. Once he understand that "shake" gets him praise and maybe food, he'll reach out to shake hands at every opportunity.

tables, which are often made of stainless steel. The combination of height and a cold, slippery surface makes dogs think more about stability than about what's happening to their feet. "A high table is a great tool," says Dr. Cox. "I know

3

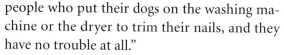

people who put their dogs on the washing machine or the dryer to trim their nails, and they have no trouble at all."

Have a friend do the work. Another reason that dogs are so cooperative at the vet's is that they're unsure about the whole situation. Dogs are big on routine and hierarchy, both of which get confused when they're away from home. The resulting uncertainty puts them off-guard, which makes it much easier to trim their nails or check their feet, says Dr. Cox. You can achieve the same result by trimming their nails away from home or even by asking (or bribing) a friend to do the work.

Practice young, practice often. Dogs are naturally protective of their feet, but they can learn to accept claw clipping and simple exams when their owners regularly handle their feet, preferably starting when they're young, says Warren Liddell, D.V.M., a veterinarian in Norwich, New York. He recommends touching, rubbing, and holding the feet for a few seconds every day. Gently press your fingers between the toes. Squeeze the pads. Spread the feet and feel around. Get your dog accustomed to the idea

that foot touches aren't a sign of uncomfortable things to come. The more gentle contact he experiences, the more likely he'll be to accept pedicures and exams as he gets older.

FAST FIX Dogs get very nervous when there's uncertainty in their lives, and objects that people take for granted, like nail trimmers, can seem foreign and frightening. A quick solution is to put the clippers somewhere that your dog will see them, like on a low table or a shelf in a bookcase, says Dr. Cox. Don't merely put them out for a few hours on the day that you're going to use them, he adds. Leave them out all the time. This will give your dog a chance to sniff, see, and generally get used to them. He still won't enjoy having his nails trimmed, but at least he'll be less nervous about the shiny, clicky object that you're holding in your hand.

Do one paw a week. Even if it were a medically sound thing to do, doctors would never want to give children an entire lifetime of vaccinations in one visit. It would be overwhelming, to say the least. The same is true of trimming a dog's nails: Doing all four paws at once can be a miserable experience, says Dr. Cox. To reduce discomfort and fear, he recommends clipping just one nail a day. With weekends off, that means you'll do one paw a week. Dogs can tolerate a little discomfort, and doing it slowly will make the process a lot more bearable.

Dogs who are used to having their feet handled from an early age, like this young mixed breed, will be blasé about the experience when they grow up.

CHAPTER TWO

BARKING AT THE MAILMAN
"See—He Went Away"

Looking at Bum, it's hard to imagine a less fearsome dog. At 7 pounds, the tiny Pomeranian looks more like a stuffed toy than a noble protector of hearth and home. But every day at about the same time, Bum undergoes a dramatic transformation. As soon as he hears the mailman's shoes on the walk, he becomes Bum the Terrible, Bum the Protector. He acts as though he'd tear off the mailman's leg if he could only get through the window.

"He's been doing it since he was a little puppy," says Jackie Savard of Tupper Lake, New York. "I don't know why Bum thinks the mailman is such a threat."

Bum probably doesn't have anything personal against the mailman. He's just taking care of his own, says Nicholas Dodman, professor of behavioral pharmacology and director of the Animal Behavior Clinic at Tufts University School of Veterinary Medicine in North Grafton, Massachusetts, and author of *Dogs Behaving Badly*. Every dog

This American bulldog likes keeping an eye on things, and she doesn't miss a chance to give a warning bark. She's protecting her territory, which, from a dog's point of view, is one of the most important things she can do.

has a little watchdog in him. It's something that dogs inherit from their ancestors, who had to defend their territories and limited food supplies from trespassers.

The great thing about mailmen is that they appear to be easy targets. Here's what happens. The first time a dog heard this stranger coming up the walk, he got alarmed.

"He probably backed up a little bit at first, but one brave day, he gave a little bark," says Dodman. His owners came running to see what was causing the commotion. The mailman, of course, dropped off the mail and left. The combination of praise from his owners and the mailman's retreat makes dogs very happy. They just assume that they scared the mailman off. From then on, they feel confident that they can protect their homes from these fearsome visitors, so they keep barking.

"Mailmen, meter readers, United Parcel Service and FedEx couriers, and any other stranger who purposely heads up to the house and then looks as though he's retreating when he gets barked at is going to get the same reception," adds Judith Halliburton, a trainer and behaviorist in Albuquerque, New Mexico, and author of *Raising Rover*.

The Best Time of Day

Nearly all dogs have an instinctive urge to protect their homes, but that's not the only reason they kick up a fuss when the mail arrives. Part of it is merely anticipation. Dogs are attuned to rituals and routines to such an extent that they'd probably be called obsessive-compulsive if they were people. The mail comes every day at more or less the same time. It doesn't matter whether this event is happily anticipated or thoroughly dreaded. Dogs probably begin thinking about it when they get up in the morning, and their excitement grows as the time approaches. By the time the mailman finally arrives, they're keyed up and ready to rumble.

"It can get to be the high point of their days," Halliburton says. Dogs who spend their days alone get particularly excited because they feel as though they've been left in charge. If they don't bark like crazy and warn off intruders, who will? "They figure they're on duty should anyone approach their property."

A sofa under a window provides a great lookout. Dogs who can see what's happening outside tend to bark the most. Moving the sofa may cut down on the noise.

Suspicious Gifts

It's not only mailmen who get dogs worked up. Just as exciting is what mailmen leave behind. Mail that drops through a slot in the door has unfamiliar smells. Dogs are suspicious of new smells, especially when the smells are in their territory. They go to a lot of trouble to put their own scents where they live—by marking around the perimeter of the yard, for example. The idea that someone would come along and put another smell on top of theirs can seem downright offensive.

Some dogs go as far as to shred mail that is dropped through the slot. They don't do it often, of course. Even people who don't mind a little barking get upset when they see the monthly mortgage statement chewed into pieces. These dogs soon find themselves relegated to other rooms.

BREED SPECIFIC

All dogs are territorial, but some breeds have notably strong instincts to protect their homes. Shelties, collies, Labradors, and golden retrievers are among the noisiest barkers. Paradoxically, dogs who were bred specifically for protection, like Dobermans, Rottweilers, and German shepherds, often bark the least. It may be that they have so much confidence that they don't feel the need to bluster.

Now That You Understand...

It's commendable that dogs are sufficiently loyal to want to protect their families. But their barking can drive people nuts. Then there's the issue of bites. Dogs do get out sometimes, and about 3,000 mailmen get bitten every year.

Barking at the mailman isn't always easy to stop. The urge to protect territory goes back hundreds of thousands of years. Dogs can learn to respect the mailman, but it's going to take some time.

Tape a biscuit to the door. Dogs may be protective, but no one ever accused them of being impractical. It's amazing how quickly they'll come around when there's something in it for them. Talk to the mailman and explain the problem, Dodman recommends. Every day after that, tape a dog treat to the door or put the box on the porch. Most mailmen will be more than happy to drop something through the slot. Strangers who bring food are always welcome, and even dogs with strong protective urges will begin to relax within a few weeks.

Rearrange the furniture. Dogs can hear people long before they see them, and that's when barking usually starts. Still, you can keep them calmer by taking away the visual red flags. This may be as simple as moving a chair in front of a window that faces the walk, or pulling the blinds, or keeping your dog in a room where he can't see outside. Your dog may still bark when he hears approaching footsteps, but without the actual visual sighting, the barking is less likely to reach a full crescendo.

This golden retriever welcomes the mailman because he gets praised for bringing the mail inside to his owners—proof that rewards are better than scoldings.

Say it once, not twice. Trainers always advise people to tell their dogs "no" when they start barking. This is good advice, but only if you do it once. When your dog is barking and you keeping saying "no," it isn't daunting—it's encouraging. Your dog will think you're barking at the mailman too, Halliburton says.

FAST FIX Just as parents are the last ones to know when their teenagers are getting into trouble, people who work all day never realize how much noise their dogs are making until neighbors complain. The corollary, of course, is that it's hard to train dogs when you aren't around to catch them barking. One way to keep them quiet when you're gone is to leave the stereo on all day, with the volume cranked up. Loud music masks outside sounds. Dogs who can't hear the mailman won't have anything at which to bark.

CHAPTER THREE

BURYING BONES

Taking Care of Leftovers

Ancient dogs didn't have people around. No people meant no refrigerators, no artificial preservatives, no ready-to-eat meals, and no safes in which to keep valuables. They survived on whatever they could find or catch. If they managed to get more than they could eat in a sitting, they had to make sure it would be there when they came back to it later.

"They stored spare food by burying it," says Benjamin Hart, D.V.M., Ph.D., professor of physiology and behavior at the University of California School of Veterinary Medicine at Davis and author of *The Perfect Puppy: How to Choose Your Dog by Its Behavior.* "It was a pretty resourceful way of keeping leftovers."

Dirt may be gritty and hard on the teeth, but it's also protective. The temperature in the ground is cooler than it is in the air, so burying food helped it stay fresh longer. Buried food didn't roast in the sun. It didn't immediately get covered with flies and insects, and buzzards couldn't swipe it. All in all, burying food and juicy bones was a very good solution. So good, in fact, that people copied the idea. Until the invention of refrigeration, people stored food in cool underground cellars.

Dogs don't need to bury food anymore because they have more than enough. But when they're faced with an overabundance of rations—and for dogs, having even 1 extra bone in the yard can feel like a tremendous extravagance—they feel that old urge coming on. So they look for a secluded spot, dig a quick hole, and put some goodies away for a rainy day. Not just bones, either. Some dogs bury toys. Others bury other people's toys. More than a few folks have had to trudge into the backyard with a shovel to uncover their 3-year-old's stuffed bear or the remote control for the VCR.

Dogs don't take chances with prized possessions. They'll either bury them for safekeeping or put on their most alert, possessive expressions.

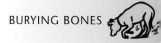

Born to Dig

Not every dog buries bones. In fact, since digging serves no practical purpose anymore, it's gradually disappearing from dogs' behavioral file cabinet. It's possible that in a few thousand years, they'll never bury anything. But in the meantime, a lot of flower beds and gardens get impromptu rototilling as dogs eagerly bury their stuff. Even dogs who have forgotten what dirt feels like will sometimes root up a lawn when they see someone else doing it.

"Dogs mimic other dogs," says Rolan Tripp, D.V.M., a veterinarian in La Mirada, California, who specializes in animal behavior. "If you have a dog who hasn't learned to bury bones or toys and he gets around one who does, he's going to be more likely to do it than a dog who doesn't have any treasure-burying friends."

Dogs imitate people almost as much as they imitate other dogs. They figure that if you're doing something, it must be fun, and they're more than willing to try it themselves. That's why there is generally an increase in digging and burying during the planting months. Dogs spend more time outside when it's warm, and they watch closely as their people bury bulbs in the fall and neat rows of seeds in the spring, says Dr. Tripp. They start thinking that they should be burying things too.

Dogs who are smart enough to dig holes to store their valuables are not always smart enough to realize that some places aren't very

This Australian shepherd loves to dig. He doesn't stop at burying bones—children's toys and the family's footwear may also go underground.

good for digging, at least from a human standpoint. No one cares when a dog buries a bone on the outer acres of a farm. A bone buried in the center of a carefully cultivated plot of Bermuda sod, however, is a problem. And one buried in the corner cushion of the sofa is an expensive disaster. Lots of dogs are perfectly willing to bury things indoors if they don't have a good place outdoors—or if they dislike getting their feet dirty. And lots of owners spend weekends repairing the damage.

Now That You Understand...

Make every bone count. Dogs bury leftovers, not the main meal. That's why a dog with

10 bones may bury 9 of them. A dog with 1 bone, on the other hand, will never let it out of his sight. When you're trying to protect your yard, only let your dog have 1 bone at a time. Throw in a few toys to keep things interesting. Then, once a week, put the bone and the toys away and bring out a new batch, Dr. Tripp suggests. Scarcity and the sense of novelty will make every bone and toy seem too important to put away.

Tie that bone down. One way to keep bones above ground is to thwart one of your dog's most powerful urges—the one that tells him to bury bones in secluded places. Take your dog's favorite bone or toy and drill a hole in one end, says Dr. Tripp. Loop a 4-foot length of chain through the hole and bolt that to a post

in the yard. Dogs who can't walk away with their prizes aren't likely to bury them. And if they do, at least it will be in the spot that you choose. The benefit for your dog, of course, is that he won't have trouble finding it later.

FAST FIX Dogs tend to bury the same bones or toys again and again, and they're invariably the ones they like least, says Dr. Hart. It would seem logical to save them some trouble—and save the yard some damage—by chucking these C-list bones in the trash. This can work if your dog actually sees you throwing the bones away, says Dr. Hart. If he doesn't, the digging will only escalate because your dog will figure that he has misplaced his buried loot and will keep digging until he finds it.

Give him a vault of his own. Rather than trying to stop dogs from burying bones and trashing the yard, sometimes it's easier to encourage them to dig—as long as it's in a spot you can live with. Pick a few square feet in the yard that will serve as an authorized digging zone, Dr. Tripp recommends. Get things rolling by burying a few things yourself while your dog watches. Or take one of his bones, throw a little dirt on top, and encourage him to go at it. As long as the location is sufficiently secluded, most dogs won't have any objection to taking over after that.

Cover his favorite spots. Some dogs will only dig in a few places. If you're lucky, covering the area with chicken wire or canvas weighted down with bricks will make it all seem like too much trouble, and he may quit digging on his own.

BREED SPECIFIC

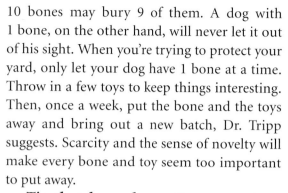

Dogs with digging in their genes are the ones most likely to bury bones and other treasures. Terriers, such as Irish terriers (left) and dachshunds, are champion diggers because it was once their job to dig deep and flush woodchucks and other rodents from their holes. Dogs from northern lands, such as huskies, also do a lot of digging, because in their native climates they had to dig down to stay warm in winter and cool in summer.

CHAPTER FOUR

CHASING CATS

They're Small and Furry, and They Look like Rabbits

Your dog may not hunt. In fact, he may be hundreds of generations removed from his nearest hunting ancestor. But his body still bears the traits of a hunting machine. Just look at those sharp incisors—they weren't designed for eating dainty bits off a china plate. And consider the eyes. They have thousands more movement receptors than people's eyes do. We see color. Dogs see action.

This kelpie mix knows a good time when he sees it, and he's standing ready for a good chase. The cat recognizes the dog's alert body language and is wisely keeping out of reach.

"Dogs have a chase drive that makes them instinctively go after anything that runs," says Rolan Tripp, D.V.M., a veterinarian in La Mirada, California, who specializes in animal behavior. And cats sure do run. Even when dogs don't have much of anything in mind, the sudden flash of feline movement sends a message to their brains: "Chase." And that's what they do.

Some dogs, of course, wouldn't get up and chase a cat on a dare. Elderly dogs and those with low-key personalities would rather sleep than chase. "Dogs who have been raised with cats since they were pups usually know that cats are just a fact," adds Dr. Tripp. "They're a whole lot less likely to chase than dogs who don't have any feline acquaintances."

Lucky for Cats

While the urge to chase prey thrives in modern dogs, the follow-up urge to kill prey has largely been extinguished. Dogs get excited by cats. They enjoy chasing cats. But once they have them cornered, they forget why they wanted them in the first place.

"Most dogs will corner a cat and then just bark out of frustration because they don't know what to do next," says Dr. Tripp.

Even when dogs have evil intentions, the result is usually the same. Cats are faster and more agile. They can leap tremendous distances and climb sheer surfaces. They usually walk away from chases without a scratch.

Expensive glassware, on the other hand, can take a beating. The usual chase scenario—a scrambling dog in pursuit of a lightning-bolt cat—involves furniture banging, glass breaking, and knee knocking. It's an instinct for pets. For humans, it's a pain in the neck.

Now That You Understand...

Raise a baby gate. Once a chase is under way, it's likely to continue until the cat is out of reach. To expedite the getaway, Dr. Tripp recommends putting a baby gate across the doorway to the kitchen or another cat-only area. Rather than putting it flush to the floor, raise it a few inches. Your cat will be able to zip underneath, leaving the bigger, clunkier dog on the other side.

BREED SPECIFIC

Dogs who have been bred for hunting, guarding, or herding, such as retrievers, Rottweilers, and Border collies, are among the most incorrigible cat chasers. So are high-energy dogs like terriers and Dalmatians. Dogs who are least likely to chase cats (or anything else) include basset hounds, Boston terriers, Great Pyrenees, and Newfoundlands.

Help her over the top. Raised gates only work when the dog is considerably bigger than the cat. When they're both the same size, put up the baby gate and rig a perch on top. This can be as simple as a section of board screwed tightly to the top. Cats are better jumpers than their canine companions, and the perch will allow them to hop up and over, leaving the dogs in their dust.

Interrupt the chase. Even though most dogs don't chase the cats they live with, some find it too much fun to give up. One way to discourage them is to keep leashes on their collars all the time. The minute they lunge, step on the leashes and make a loud noise, suggests Dr. Tripp. Stepping on the leashes arrests their forward momentum and gives them a jolt, and the loud noise makes the whole experience a little uncomfortable. Most dogs will get the hint after awhile that chasing cats has dubious payoffs.

Putting a baby gate or a piece of lattice across a doorway will stop even large dogs, like this Irish wolfhound, from bothering the cats.

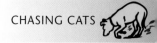

Even when they don't lose interest entirely, past experiences of leash jolts will cause them to hesitate for a few seconds—and that's all the time that most cats need to put a safe distance between them and their pursuers.

Like an ex-smoker who takes a puff, however, dogs can get hooked on cat chasing all over again if they get a chance to do it. So you'll have to keep an eye on them all the time.

Cats and dogs get along best when they've been raised together and have been encouraged to develop respect and affection for each other.

The Hustler

All dogs are not created equal. Some are big and some are small. Some are smart and some aren't so brilliant. And some move at a snail's pace while others sprint. Sprinting was the case with Abby. Abby was much less interested in chasing cats than in racing them. And she managed to put one overconfident kitty soundly in his place.

The cat was White Bear. White Bear was fast, even for a cat. He was born with extra toes. When his owner, Carol Vinnacombe of Long Beach, California, asked her veterinarian if her kitten would have any health problems, he solemnly replied that White Bear would be fine, but he'd be very quick on his feet.

White Bear was fully aware of his gift. His favorite game, in fact, was Bait the Dog. "He walks into the room, surveys the dogs, and meows," Carol says. "If that doesn't work, he's not above batting at them with his paws." Carol's two Dalmatians always rose to the challenge, but they never managed to get close before White Bear would dive under the baby gate at the door.

Then Abby joined the family. White Bear wasted no time trying to get a game going with the lanky grey dog. He waved his paw in the air. Abby stood up. White Bear shot off. But when he skidded to the gate, the shocked cat found that Abby was already there and waiting.

It wasn't a fluke. Abby, it turns out, was a greyhound. And not just any greyhound. She was a retired racer who had spent the first 4 years of her life on the track. White Bear's little scam was like a neighborhood hustler challenging a stranger to a one-on-one game of basketball—only to discover that the stranger was Michael Jordan. For the first time in his life, White Bear had been slam-dunked.

Lucky for him, Abby didn't know what she was getting into, either. Once she'd won the race, she just turned and walked away. White Bear still plays his game sometimes, but finally someone besides the Dalmatians knows the agony of defeat.

CHAPTER FIVE

CHEWING SHOES

They Smell Good and Are Easy to Reach

Human feet have about half a million sweat glands, which are always secreting moisture. When feet are tucked into hot, humid shoes, the glands can release $1/2$ pint of sweat a day. The perspiration, in turn, is loaded with human scents, and that's hard for any dog to resist.

Adult dogs generally understand that just because something smells good doesn't mean they have to chew it. But when they're young, dogs respond to shoes in the same way they respond to anything that gets their attention—by putting them in their mouths, says Kay Cox, Ph.D., an animal-behavior consultant in Gilbert, Arizona.

Added to this natural attraction is that fact that puppies go through a teething phase. Few things make their gums feel better than working over a nice pair of loafers.

It sometimes seems that dogs' interest in shoes is directly related to the cost: The more expensive the shoes, the more likely dogs are to leave them in tatters. But they really don't have a preference, says Gregory Bogard, D.V.M., a veterinarian in Tomball, Texas. They can't tell which shoes come from Saks Fifth Avenue and which come from K-Mart. All they know is that shoes smell exciting and are worth an exploratory chew or two.

"To your dog, that personal smell is the next best thing to you," explains Dr. Cox. In fact, dogs rarely chew up the shoes of people whom they dislike. "If they really hate someone, they might tear their shoes up," she adds. "But most dogs really want to be close to the familiar, pleasant smell of their owners."

Easy to Reach

People always wonder why puppies—and, less often, older dogs—focus on shoes and ignore other human possessions that are also loaded

A smelly tennis shoe left outside to air is too much temptation for this Border collie to resist. She has to explore it—with her teeth as well as her nose.

with scents. There are a few reasons for this. Partly, it's the intensity of the smell. A couch cushion will have some human scents, but nowhere near the concentration of a hot, humid pair of pumps.

More important, shoes are singularly convenient. When people leave home for the day, it's normal for dogs to explore a bit. They'll sniff around the living room, the bedrooms, and the closets. Sooner or later, they'll come across a pair of shoes. They're right on the floor, they smell great, and they're just the right size. They may decide that their search is over and commence digging in, says Dr. Bogard.

The Joy of Leather

Some dogs will chew rubber galoshes if that's all they can find. But given the choice, most go for leather shoes. Leather is made from cowhide. Despite all the treatments and tanning and dyes that go into shoe-making, dogs still recognize leather as a substance that's darn close to food.

An added bonus is that leather gets softer and tastier the more dogs chew it, says Dr. Cox. "Once they've started to wear it away, leather massages their gums just like rawhide does. There's a good taste, a good smell, and great mouth appeal, too."

Leather shoes with tassels are especially popular, Dr. Bogard adds. "They're like great-smelling chew toys with tails," he says. "That makes them very hard to resist."

When his folks are away, this German shepherd likes to raid the closets in search of shoes. They smell of his people, and that makes him feel less alone.

Dogs who are into shoes usually aren't very selective, however. Canvas shoes aren't as toothsome as leather, but they're easier to rip into shreds. Dogs enjoy getting that kind of results. Fuzzy slippers are good, too. For one thing, they're warm, which means they cause the feet to exude additional dog-attracting moisture. Plus, all of that faux fur is more than a canine hunter's heart can resist. "I don't think there are many dogs who really think those slippers are alive, but they have a lot of fun pretending they are," says Dr. Bogard.

Now That You Understand...

Put in an insert. Since it's mainly the smell of human feet that makes shoes so tempting, you can make them less so by using shoe inserts. Inserts absorb most of the odors, leaving the shoes themselves relatively scent-free, says Rolan Tripp, D.V.M., a veterinarian in La Mirada, California, who specializes in animal behavior. Of course, you have to remember to remove the inserts when you get home. Otherwise, your shoes will smell as tempting as they always do.

ONLY THE BEST

A decade ago, people going out of town for a few days often left their dogs in boarding kennels, bare-boned establishments that didn't provide much more than a "hot and a cot." But in the last few years, upper-end boarding facilities have begun providing canine guests with everything from organized play sessions to water beds to color TV.

Carol Boerio-Croft, owner of Cozy Inn Pet Resort and Spa in Stahlstown, Pennsylvania, is used to special requests. Some people drop off recipes for gourmet meals. Others bring their dogs' beds and linens. And nearly everyone brings along their dogs' favorite toys.

Some dogs seem a little too pampered, she adds. One regular client always brings along an expensive, almost-new high-heel pump for her dog to chew. "I'm sure pets appreciate the comforts of home," Boerio-Croft says, "but I'd hate to have a dog accustomed to those perks getting too close to my closet."

FAST FIX An easy way to make shoes less appealing is to cover the human scent with a scent that dogs dislike. Dr. Tripp recommends using medicated—and scented—shoe inserts. Or you can spray the insides of the shoes with mint breath spray. Most dogs dislike the smell of mint and will stay away from it. Deodorants containing alum are also a good choice, he says. Use a roll-on deodorant, and put a heavy layer of it on the footpad. If you're using inserts as well, roll it on both sides, he advises.

Teach the difference between shoes and toys. It's rare for dogs to deliberately target shoes or other human possessions. They're just attracted by the scents, and then their natural chewing instincts take over. You have to teach them the difference between shoes and toys, says Dr. Bogard.

Several times a day, bring out a tempting shoe and put it on the floor. Put one of your dog's toys a few feet away. Watch as he heads for the goodies. If he approaches the shoe, tell him "no." When he shifts gears and moves toward the toy, tell him "good boy!" Keep practicing. Periodically move the shoe and the toy farther and farther apart. Most dogs will learn the difference within a few weeks, says Dr. Bogard.

In the early days of training, of course, you'll want to remember to keep your shoes out of reach, Dr. Bogard adds. Young dogs get bored easily and are going to explore. You don't want them to find anything good when you're not around to watch them.

CHAPTER SIX

PAWING BEFORE LYING DOWN
A Comforting Ritual

Everyone has a little bedtime ritual. For children, it's toothbrushing, stories, and lights-out. For their parents, it might be pillow fluffing or putting on satin pajamas. For dogs, it's pawing the ground—or the carpet—before settling in.

"Some dogs' routines are so precise that you can tell even before they start moving what they're getting ready to do," says Emily Weiss, curator of behavior and research at Sedgwick County Zoo in Wichita, Kansas. "You can just see that look in the eye that says, 'Okay, I'm going to turn around four times, paw six times, lie down, sigh, and fall right to sleep.'"

Bowser Was Here

It's only in the last hundred years that dogs have had the opportunity to lie down on fluffy, well-laundered, and comfortable beds. Before that, they had to make their sleeping arrangements in all sorts of rugged, drafty places. They would rearrange the ground a bit in order to create comfortable hollows. It was a bit warmer than sleeping on the surface, and it allowed them to contour the ground to accommodate four legs and a tail, Weiss says.

This kelpie loves her foam bedding—but every time she snuggles down for a rest, she destroys a bit more of it with her paws. It has to be replaced regularly.

A thick pile carpet or a plaid cedar bed doesn't need this sort of treatment, but dogs are creatures of habit. They tend to do the same things they've always done. Every dog develops a slightly different set of bedtime rituals, and for the most part, they'll follow these rituals every time they lie down. "Once they get in the habit of pawing or scratching or circling around before they lie down, they're going to always want to do it," says Vint Virga, D.V.M., a veterinarian at the College of Veterinary Medicine at Cornell University in Ithaca, New York.

Comfort and ritual are only part of the story. Another reason for pawing is that dogs are territorial animals, which means they stake out and claim areas that they consider theirs, says

A freshly dug hole makes a bed that is perfectly tailored for this terrier mix. It is shaped to his body and provides protection from the elements.

Weiss. One way of marking territory is to scratch at the ground. In the wild, dogs who happened by would see the scratch marks and know that the place was occupied. They'd smell the marks, too. Dogs have scent glands in their paws. Pawing at the carpet is one way of depositing their personal scent, she explains.

"I had two males who took turns rumpling up a bath mat," says Betty Fisher, an animal behaviorist and trainer in San Diego and co-author of *So Your Dog's Not Lassie*. "One would go in the bathroom, wad it up, then come back out. Later, the other one would do the same thing." Both dogs wanted to be the last to claim the mat, even though neither of them wanted to sleep on it, she says.

Female dogs may be somewhat more likely than males to paw before lying down, especially if they happen to be pregnant. It's because they have a biological urge to prepare a safe, comfortable nest for their puppies, explains Dr. Virga.

Feels Good to Scratch

From the time they're puppies, dogs will scratch and dig just about anywhere—on the carpet, in the garden, even on linoleum floors. They're not really trying to make a bed in all of these places. They just enjoy scratching. "It feels great on their paws," Weiss says. "If it's hot outside, they'll scratch and get a little cool dirt under their nails. Before long, they're hooked."

This is why some dogs spend an inordinate amount of time pawing the carpet or their beds before lying down. They don't need to make things more comfortable than they already are. They're just enjoying the activity. And since they find it relaxing, it's a natural prelude to taking a nap. "They don't necessarily have a goal in mind," Weiss says. "They do it because it feels good."

Now That You Understand...

It's rare for dogs to do any real damage during their pre-nap pawing. Even though their instincts are telling them to make a comfortable hollow, all they're really doing is following an age-old ritual and going through the motions. But there are exceptions. Some dogs have every intention of making a real bed, and they'll shred cushions and wear away patches of carpet in order to get it just so, Fisher says. Since you can't stop them from pawing, you'll have to work out ways to accommodate the instinct without sacrificing the house.

Give them a bed of their own. This is by far the simplest solution. Most dogs appreciate having a bed that's theirs and theirs alone. Even when they're reluctant to use it at first, the gradual accretion of personal smells will make it part of their territory, and they'll want to go there when it's time to sleep, Weiss says. Dog beds are made to withstand a lot of abuse, and most have washable covers as well.

Buy a loose-fill bed. As far as comfort is concerned, it doesn't matter all that much what kind of bed you buy. To give the most pawing satisfaction, however, you may want to get a bed that's made from loose fill—from cedar chips, for example—rather than a solid mattress. This gives dogs the opportunity to move the filling around when they paw, which is closer to what they'd experience naturally.

This bullterrier mix loves her beanbag bed. The filling is loose, which means she can paw at it and rearrange it to her own satisfaction.

Put the bed where your dog will use it. No one enjoys spending $50 for a comfortable bed, only to watch their dog give it an indifferent sniff before curling up on a corner of the couch. Since dogs are intensely attuned to territory, you'll need to be accommodating in finding the best place to put the bed, Fisher says. If there's one spot where your dog always settles down to sleep, you'll want to put the bed as close to that spot as possible. And you'll want to keep it in the same area where people spend most of their time, since those are the places that dogs consider home. Dogs like feeling protected when they sleep, and they're more likely to use a bed that's in a corner, she adds.

FAST FIX If your dog has one spot where he always sleeps, you may want to put down a blanket or a soft throw rug. "Putting down throws means I still get to have a nice-looking room, and my dogs have something comfy to sink their paws into," Fisher says. "My dogs are happy, and I don't have to replace the carpets."

CHAPTER SEVEN

DIGGING

A Talent They're Born With

Some dogs have practical reasons for digging. It gets them under the fence. They're convinced that there is something underground worth having. Or they simply want to create a comfy, climate-controlled bed in which they can curl up and go to sleep.

Then there are dogs who couldn't care less about practicality. They dig for one reason and one reason only: It's a heck of a lot of fun. For them, digging is the canine equivalent of sailing on the ocean and enjoying the salty air. They love the smell of freshly turned dirt and the way it feels under their paws. They enjoy the feeling of exhilaration that comes from tossing clouds of dirt behind them. Digging is their sport and their hobby. It requires no special equipment, and they can do it any time and just about anywhere.

Have Skills, Need Job

The reason that dogs are attracted to dirt in the first place comes down to one thing: instinct. Long before L.L. Bean started making cedar-filled beds, dogs dug themselves dens, both for sleeping and for a secure place to raise their pups. They dug to catch burrowing prey and to bury leftovers. Digging was one of the few useful tools they had at their disposal, and they used it often, says Inger Martens, a trainer and behaviorist in Los Angeles and author of *Paws for a Minute*.

Aside from searching around in the garden for treasures or making the occasional great escape, dogs don't have many real uses for digging anymore. That's fine for some dogs and some breeds. Greyhounds and Great Danes, for example, were never much into digging anyway. But others can't leave it alone.

"Terriers were bred to control vermin and snakes, and dachshunds were badger dogs," says

Dogs will sometimes start digging when they see someone else doing it. The smell of all that newly dug earth stimulates ancient instincts, and they can't resist trying it themselves.

James H. Sokolowski, D.V.M., Ph.D., a veterinarian in Vernon, California. "For hundreds of years, breeders picked the dogs that had the most enthusiasm for digging. You can't just turn that off."

Instinct is a powerful force. Add to it generations of specialized breeding, and you have a lot of dogs who will always find a way and a place to dig, even when there's nothing to dig for.

Young and Foolish

Dogs who are destined to dig usually hit their strides between the ages of 3 months and 3 years, says Martens. Some get started after watching another dog do it, or even after watching their owners in the garden. Others don't need any more inspiration than an afternoon of boredom and the desire to try something new. It doesn't take much to get them started. They'll paw at a cricket on the grass, for example, and that leads to more pawing, and pretty soon the entire yard is filled with craters. At that point, they're usually hooked and aren't going to give it up easily, Martens says.

"Dogs need to burn off steam and calories just as people do," Martens adds. "And no matter what else you may think of it, you've got to admit that digging is a great workout."

The Hole Story

Stopping dogs from digging requires counterintelligence and guerilla tactics. You'll never stop them from doing it until you figure out why they're doing it. You can tell a lot from where they're digging and the types of holes they dig.

Dogs dig different sorts of holes for different reasons. This Australian shepherd always digs at the fence line because he wants to get out and explore.

• Holes by the fence mean that dogs are digging to escape—sometimes because something is intriguing them, but mainly because they're bored and looking for action, Martens says. Pets who haven't been neutered, of course, have more compelling reasons to get out.

• Holes by the house are a sign that dogs are lonely and want to get inside where the people are, says Dr. Sokolowski.

• Shallow holes scattered around the yard usually indicate that a dog is trying to get comfortable. They're a type of thermoregulation: Holes are cool in summer and warm in winter, says Dr. Sokolowski. Supplying a wading pool filled with cool water or, in winter, giving dogs a sheltered place with a warm bed will often stop them from digging. These dogs are just trying to get comfortable, and they'd be perfectly content to not have to labor for their comfort.

Now That You Understand...

It's quite easy to recognize dogs who dig just for the thrill of it. They look happy. In addition, dogs who have a specific purpose in mind usually dig when they're alone. Happy diggers, on the other hand, will do it any time. In fact, they may be more likely to dig when people are around, because they want to share their excitement.

It's not impossible to teach dogs to leave the dirt alone, but it's an uphill fight—and the dogs are usually the winners. Compromise is usually a better choice than confrontation.

"We all want our dogs to have nice, complete lives," says Dr. Sokolowski. "If digging is their passion, you can help them find a way to do it that doesn't destroy your property."

1. Pick an acceptable spot. Unless your yard is the size of a postage stamp, there's sure to be a place where you wouldn't mind having a few holes. It can't be too far out of the way, however, because dogs avoid places where they feel isolated, says Dr. Sokolowski. It has to be a place

With their sensitive noses, dogs can detect intriguing smells even under snow—and snow is easier to dig than dirt.

where they feel comfortable. Look at the holes your dog has already dug to get clues about her choice of terrain.

2. Bury something good. Dogs aren't going to start digging just because you point to a spot and say, "Dig." You have to make it worth their while. Dig a small hole yourself and bury a bone or one of your dog's favorite toys, advises Dr. Sokolowski. Let her watch while you do it. This will give her the idea, and it won't take long before she notices a familiar, intriguing scent wafting up from the ground. Then she's on her own.

3. Cheer her on. Once she starts tunneling, encourage her. Act excited. Maybe get down on all fours and dig a little yourself. Enthusiasm is contagious. Your excitement will let her know that she's on to something, and she'll keep digging to get more of that good energy.

FAST FIX Your dog may or may not catch on to the fact that you want her to dig in this one place and not somewhere else. If she keeps returning to her favorite holes, you may have to booby-trap them by filling them with rocks and topping them off with a healthy dusting of ground red pepper. Dogs dislike the smell of red pepper, and they certainly don't like digging through rocks, Dr. Sokolowski says.

EATING GRASS

Better Than Antacids

Nearly every dog eats grass sometimes, and some dogs eat it all the time. You would think that veterinarians would have a pretty good idea by now of why they do it. But they don't, mainly because no one has figured out how to ask dogs two important questions: "Do you like the taste?" and "If it tastes so good, why do you throw it up?"

"I swear sometimes that my dog is an Angus," says Marty Becker, D.V.M., a veterinarian in Bonners Ferry, Idaho, and coauthor of *Chicken Soup for the Pet Lover's Soul.* "He lies out in the yard and grazes just like a cow." He doesn't get sick, either, Dr. Becker adds. He just munches happily, then closes his eyes and takes a little nap.

These beagles are enjoying a grassy snack. It has a fresh taste they like, and it doubles as medicine when they're feeling ill.

"Dogs explore their worlds with their noses and mouths," Dr. Becker says. "And there's the grass, attractive, sweet-smelling, with an appealing texture; and it's ever-so-accessible on the ground. Why not eat it?"

A Craving for Greens

Dogs are remarkably flexible in their tastes. They'll polish off a bowl of dried dog food, then walk over to see if there's anything good in the trash. If they're still hungry, they'll wander upstairs to see what's in the cat's box. Basically, they'll eat, or at least sample, whatever they find in front of them.

There's a good reason for their liberal tastes. Unlike cats, who evolved solely as hunters, dogs survived by scavenging. When they couldn't catch live prey, which was a lot of the time, they'd eat the ancient equivalent of roadkill. They didn't care too much if had been lying in the sun for a week or was half-buried under old leaves. It was food, and they weren't going to pass it up. When meat wasn't on the table, they'd root around for tender leafy stalks, or roots, or an old polished bone. They simply weren't fussy, and dogs today haven't gotten

CALL FOR HELP

It's not exactly pleasant when your dog throws up wads of grass on the living room carpet, but he's probably not too sick, either. Once he gets rid of the grass and whatever happens to be irritating his stomach, he'll probably start feeling better soon. Dogs who throw up three or more times in a day, however, need to see a veterinarian, whether or not they've been eating grass, says Sheila McCullough, D.V.M., clinical assistant professor at the University of Illinois College of Veterinary Medicine at Urbana-Champaign.

any fussier. They're predisposed to like just about everything.

In addition, there's some evidence that dogs get cravings for certain foods, says Dottie LaFlamme, D.V.M., Ph.D., a veterinary nutritionist with the Purina company in St. Louis. It's possible that dogs occasionally get a hankering for greens, just as people sometimes go to bed dreaming about mashed potatoes and meat loaf.

It's not as strange as it may sound. Grass was part of their ancestors' regular diets. Dogs are omnivores, which means they eat meat as well as plants. They don't need grassy nutrients any more because most commercial dog foods are nutritionally complete. But dogs aren't nutritionists. They don't know or care that they've already gotten their vitamin or mineral quotients from a bowl of kibble. Their instincts tell them that grass is good, so they eat it. Besides, there's a world of difference between satisfying

the minimal nutritional requirements and having a great meal. And for many dogs, a mouthful of grass clearly tastes great. It's like a salad—they eat some, then want more.

Under the Weather

Even dogs who usually don't eat grass will head straight for the nearest patch when they're feeling sick. They'll gobble a few mouthfuls, retch, and then throw up, or at least try to. Veterinarians still aren't sure if dogs eat grass because their stomachs are upset or if their stomachs get upset after they eat grass. Dr. Becker suspects it's the former, because dogs who are energetic and perky seem to be able to eat grass without getting sick afterward. It seems likely that there's something in grass that does stimulate the urge to vomit.

"The stomach has all kinds of neuro-receptors that respond to what dogs ingest," says Dr. LaFlamme. "They react to acidity, chemical content, and textures. I think the texture of the grass has something like a tickle effect on the stomach, which induces vomiting."

This tummy tickle may explain why healthy dogs can eat grass without getting sick. They take a mouthful, chew it thoroughly and swallow, then reach down for some more. Dogs who are sick, however, appear almost desperate for the grass. They don't chew it carefully or savor the taste. They gobble it. Without the chewing, those prickly little stalks hit their stomachs all at once. This may be what stimulates the urge to throw it all back up—along with whatever was irritating their stomachs in the first place.

"They can't stick their fingers down their throats or ask for syrup of ipecac," Dr. Becker adds. "Eating grass is something that works." And once dogs find something that works, they tend to stick with it.

Now That You Understand...

Keep the grass clean. Unless your dog is in the habit of regurgitating grass on the dining room floor, there's no reason to worry about it, says Dr. Becker. Dogs have been eating grass for thousands or tens of thousands of years, and there's no evidence at all that it's bad for them. That isn't the case, however, when grass has been treated with insecticides, herbicides, or other chemicals. Most products say on the label whether they're dangerous for pets. In any event, you should certainly keep dogs away from grass soon after chemicals have been applied. Most products break down fairly quickly, but they can be quite dangerous if your dog eats them while they're fresh.

Stay away if it's green. You can control what goes on your own lawn, but there's no telling what neighbors put on theirs. Often, the prettiest lawns are the ones that have been most heavily treated with chemicals, says Dr. Becker. Your dog will be better off grazing on lawns that look a little grungier.

Make a broccoli shake. It's just a theory at this point, but some veterinarians believe that dogs eat grass because they're not getting enough fiber in their diets. You may want to buy a higher-fiber food—pet foods for "seniors" generally have the most. These foods can be expensive, however, so you may want to look for

Grass is harmless to dogs, but herbicides and insecticides are not. Try to keep dogs away from grass that you know or suspect has been treated.

other ways to supplement your dog's diet. Most dogs don't care for raw vegetables, but you can run some broccoli or green beans through the blender, adding chicken or beef broth for flavor. Or add a sprinkling of bran to their food.

FAST FIX It's pretty obvious when dogs are feeling sick. When their hangdog, under-the-weather expressions are accompanied by diarrhea or vomiting, an upset stomach is probably the reason. A quick way to soothe an upset stomach is to give dogs a little Pepto-Bismol, says Dr. Becker. Veterinarians recommend giving about half of a tablespoon for every 15 pounds of weight, two or three times a day.

CHAPTER NINE

LICKING FACES

A Show of Love

Dogs use their long tongues for mopping up lunch crumbs, removing mud from their feet, and cleaning their privates. And yet, when they give our faces sloppy licks, there's something endearing about it. Apart from occasional attempts to retrieve bits of glazed doughnut from our chins, dogs lick us because they like us. It isn't a kiss, but it's close.

Almost as soon as they're born, dogs experience the soft warmth of their mothers' tongue, which bathes them with maternal affection, says Gary Landsberg, D.V.M., an animal behaviorist and veterinarian in Toronto, Ontario, Canada. The licking never really stops after that. Mothers take advantage of their puppies' relative immobility during nursing to lick them clean. They also lick their bottoms to jump-start their impulses to relieve themselves.

Puppies do their share of licking too. They lick older dogs' chins and faces to greet them and show respect. And when they're hungry—and puppies are perpetually in search of something to eat—

Dogs lick people's faces to show their respect, though some people aren't as appreciative as others.

licking their mother will sometimes stimulate her to regurgitate a meal, which the puppies regard as an appetizing lunch, says Benjamin Hart, D.V.M., Ph.D., director of the Center for Animal Behavior at the University of California School of Veterinary Medicine at Davis. As dogs get older, they lick each other less often, but they never quit entirely. At the very least, in the absence of hands and hairbrushes, they do each other's hair with their tongues.

A Sign of Respect

Dogs don't lick people because they're hoping for a hot meal. They lick because we're their parents, or at least the head folks in the house. Even when dogs are old, gray, and grizzled, they see themselves in some ways as being our children, and a lick shows how much they respect us, says Dr. Hart.

You can tell a little bit about your dog's personality by how much licking she does, says Dr. Hart. Dogs who are very bold or independent are restrained with their licking because they don't feel as though there is anyone they have to win over. Outgoing, sociable dogs, on the other hand, lick everyone all the time.

Friendly, sociable breeds, like these young golden retrievers, tend to lick people much more than reserved and independent dogs do.

We play a role in all this licking too. It doesn't take dogs very long to learn that laying a wet one on the cheek is a great way to get cooed over and rubbed the right way. So in a way, the instinct to lick is both ancient and immediate; dogs do it naturally, and we encourage them to do it more.

Now That You Understand...

People are never sure how to react to licks. The first emotion is generally "Aw, shucks," closely followed by "Yuck." Imagine where that tongue has been! But it's not as unhygienic as it seems. At worst, says Dr. Landsberg, dog licks are like wiping your face with a slightly dirty washcloth. Not exactly cleansing, but hardly worth worrying about. In fact, there's some evidence that it may be good for you.

In generations past, long before Betadine and antibiotics, people noticed how dogs always licked their own wounds. They suspected that licking may be good for people too. They weren't entirely wrong. Dog saliva does have a mild antibacterial effect, says Dr. Hart, that is certainly good for dogs and doesn't do any harm to people.

As for catching a canine cold, it's not going to happen. Most diseases are only passed within species—from dog to dog or person to person, but not between the two groups. The main exception to this is people with weakened immune systems, who are more susceptible to all sorts of illness, including those passed by overly affectionate dogs.

FAST FIX Dogs have flexible spines, long tongues, and an utter lack of regard for social niceties, which becomes evident when they settle down in public and give their nether regions a long, unctuous licking. It's noisy to listen to and unpleasant to watch, but it's well-intentioned. "People wash, but dogs lick," says Sheila McCullough, D.V.M., clinical assistant professor at the University of Illinois College of Veterinary Medicine at Urbana-Champaign.

Dogs usually don't spend more than a few minutes licking their privates. When they spend longer than that, it's probably because they're uncomfortable. Their bellies and groins have less fur than the rest of their bodies, so those areas are vulnerable to irritation. In addition, dogs often get swollen anal sacs—small sacs inside the anus that contain a fluid used for scent-marking—which make them itchy. A long licking gives relief.

CHAPTER TEN

PROTECTING EMPTY FOOD BOWLS

Memories of Lean Times

I f there's one thing that brings out dogs' possessive tendencies, it's food. Among any group of mammals, from lion prides to wolf packs, nothing affects survival as much as getting enough to eat—and eating it before someone else does.

Some dogs have elevated their protective instincts to a speed sport. They hunker over their dishes and inhale the food to ensure that no one else gets a crack at it. All the while, they look around furtively for food thieves. Some get downright aggressive, giving a guttural growl if anyone gets close.

The bowl doesn't have to be full to trigger protective feelings, adds Joanne Howl, D.V.M., a veterinarian in West River, Maryland. "Lots of dogs see their bowls as their possessions," she explains. "They probably imagine that food might appear there at any time. So the bowl isn't just any possession—it's highly prized."

It's not just the bowl they're protecting, but the space around it, Dr. Howl adds. This is due in part to what is called their denning instinct. Dogs in the wild always lived in cozy, enclosed spaces called dens. A den might have been a cave or an abandoned shed. Or it could have been a hollow in the ground, surrounded by trees. Dogs viewed their dens as their castles, and they didn't welcome strangers coming around. So they did whatever they had to do to protect their space.

In addition, dogs like a little peace and quiet when they eat. It's their way of making sure no one gets close enough to steal their food. They may get cranky when

This Labrador is keeping a wary eye on her bowl, just in case anyone tries to make a raid. The fact that it's empty doesn't seem to make a difference.

Friendship never extends to the food bowl. Even dogs who normally get along fine, like these two mixed breeds, will get defensive whenever one approaches the other's bowl.

there's too much activity around their food bowls, even when mealtimes are a long way off. "For a dog, an empty dinner dish is just a meal waiting to happen," says Dr. Howl.

Family Competition

There's nothing like a little sibling rivalry to stir up food-guarding feelings. Dogs who live with other dogs may view each other as competitors for food, treats, toys, and attention, says Robin Kovary, director of the American Dog Trainers Network in New York City and author of *From Good Puppy to Great Dog!* This makes sense because dogs know what other dogs are thinking. They instinctively understand that their food is up for grabs if they don't grab it first.

Competition among dogs has a way of extending to other members of the family. That's when mild protective feelings escalate to baleful glances, growls, or worse. At that point, your dog doesn't view you as a benign and friendly presence. She sees you as a competing appetite.

Hungry, Not Greedy

Some dogs guard their dishes simply because they're not getting enough to eat, Kovary says. Even though about a third of dogs in the United States are overweight, some dogs still aren't getting all the calories they need, because their owners are overly concerned about keeping them trim. Dogs who are truly ravenous won't be on their best behavior, and they certainly won't let their food bowls out of sight, if they can help it.

Even when a dog's stomach isn't growling, she may protect the bowl if she has gone through lean times. This tends to be an issue for dogs who spent their early months as strays, Kovary says. Like children of the Depression, they remember what it's like to be hungry, and they aren't going to let it happen again.

Since every dog needs a different number of calories, the only way to be sure that your dog is getting enough is to watch her ribs. They should be almost visible, but nicely padded. If they're too prominent—or, conversely, if you can't see them at all—you should make some adjustments to the amount of food that you pour into the bowl.

Now That You Understand...

Put the bowl in the middle of a big room. Dogs are most possessive of their bowls when they're put in small, confined places, says Kovary. It's a matter of perception as well as practicality. Dogs who feel crowded get uneasy because they suspect that there is going to be competition for this very valuable resource. And small places are easy to guard. A big, open space, however, would be a chore to protect. Most dogs won't bother.

Move the bowl around. Since it's not only the bowl but also the space around it that dogs protect, Dr. Howl recommends moving the bowl all the time—Monday in the kitchen, Tuesday on the porch, and so on. When dogs eat in different places every day, they attach less importance to the bowl than to the food that's in it.

Make the bowl vanish. No one wants to be washing dog dishes all the time, which is why bowls tend to become permanent fixtures on the floor. Dogs look at them and think, "Mine." You can make the bowl seem incidental and unimportant just by picking it up after every meal, Dr. Howl says.

Toy poodles and other small dogs tend to bond more closely with people than with dogs, whom they see as competitors for affection as well as for food.

> ### BREED SPECIFIC
>
> German shepherds, Rottweilers, and other dogs used for protection can get very possessive of their food bowls—not only because they have assertive personalities but also because they often get suspicious of interlopers. On the other hand, dogs bred for teamwork, such as retrievers, don't get hung up on what belongs to whom. Sharing is in their genes.

Have them work for food. No matter how protective dogs feel inside, they only express it when they're sure they can get away with it. You don't want to make life too easy for them, Kovary says. She recommends making them work before they get fed.

For example, have your dog sit before you put the bowl on the floor. Let her wait there for a minute. Or make her lie down or come when you call or do anything else that you say. This is your dog's "payment" for the meal. Dogs who have to earn their privileges know better than to be grouchy, because they understand from whose hands the food flows.

FAST FIX Probably the quickest way to make your dog less protective is to drop a small treat in the bowl every time she is eating. Make it something special—a morsel of cheese or a piece of hot dog, says Kovary. Your dog will start viewing you more as a waiter than a competitor. In fact, rather than looking suspicious when you approach the bowl, she's going to get downright excited.

CHAPTER ELEVEN

ROLLING IN STINKY THINGS

It's about Bragging Rights

Every morning, Laura Whittaker and her Labrador, Stormy, climb the hill behind her house in Franklin, New York, to feed the horses. Whittaker carries a mug of coffee and a couple of carrots. Stormy runs ahead, happy to see a new day.

It's a peaceful, idyllic time—until Stormy spies a fresh pile of horse dung and decides to take a roll. The invigorated but filthy dog then proceeds to run in circles, coming dangerously close to his disgusted owner as they head back home. Laura goes in the house with her coffee. Stormy stays on the porch.

He's certainly not the only one. Dogs seem driven to roll in filth—the dirtier and smellier, the better. Collectively, they've spent years on the porch because their owners don't want them tracking their odoriferous business inside. The dogs, of course, don't seem to think they stink. If anything, they act happier the dirtier they get, and they're always eager to share their scents with the people they love.

Smells like Home

No one knows for sure why dogs roll in stinky things, but people who study animal behavior have some pretty good hunches.

"My best guess is that dogs like to mark themselves with their territory," says Patricia McConnell, Ph.D., a certified applied animal behaviorist in Black Earth, Wisconsin. "A dog wearing a bit of woodchuck carcass or horse poop on his neck and shoulders is a lot like a guy wearing a big gold chain around his neck. It says something about him and where he lives, something like, 'I'm a dog of means; I own the territory with all this great stuff.'"

It's hard for people to understand how anyone, even a dog, could rate the value of his territory according to its riches of cow pies. This is one of those situations that illustrates how completely different dogs and people are. People appreciate things that are clean and fresh. Dogs like things that are old and smelly.

For this elkhound, happiness is a dead fish on a beach. He's making sure to coat himself with the smell.

Smells that dogs find delectable are often the ones that make people reel. About all you can do is give them a bath and keep them outside until the stench wears off.

There may be a good reason for their off-putting tastes. Dogs have spent eons scrounging for food. It's possible that even the hint of a good meal triggers a sense of elation, says Tony Buffington, D.V.M., Ph.D., professor of clinical nutrition at the Ohio State University College of Veterinary Medicine in Columbus. Out of necessity, they may have developed a unique appreciation for anything that's remotely edible. A week-old carcass certainly qualifies. So does a fish washed up on shore. Even the presence of deer or cow dung suggests that there's a potential meal somewhere in the neighborhood.

Smells Good to Me

Then again, there may be a simpler reason why dogs enjoy coating themselves with horrid things, one that has nothing to do with survival and everything to do with taste. It's possible, explains Dr. McConnell, that they roll in dung, carcasses, and pond scum because they like the smell. Not just a little, but enough to want to carry it around with them, just as people enjoy dabbing themselves with Chanel No. 5.

"Smell is such a primal sense, it's hard to account for who likes what," says Dr. McConnell. Just as some people enjoy Limburger cheese, dogs may revel in smells that most of us find objectionable. It's hard to criticize their tastes, because they have millions more scent receptors than we do. Our own senses of smell are barely functional compared to theirs. It's possible that they detect pleasing odors of which people are completely unaware.

"I put on gardenia because I like it," says Dr. McConnell. "And when dogs put on dead fish or cow pies, I have no doubt that it smells really good to them. It might even impress their friends."

Now That You Understand...

Dogs have been rolling in dirty things for as long as they've been dogs. It's as much a part of who they are as their barks and wagging tails. They aren't going to quit doing it just because people want them to. Even professional trainers have a hard time making them stop. About all that you can hope to achieve is keeping them away from temptation—and, when that fails, knocking down the odor enough that they're bearable to be around.

Neutralize the smell. Baths are fine for eliminating a little bit of doggy smell, but they won't do a thing for a dog who has rolled on an old catfish. If anything, washing them seems to raise the scent. A better choice may be an odor neutralizer. Available in pet supply stores, these contain ingredients that break down bad odors chemically. Dr. McConnell recommends a spray called Skunk Kleen. "I don't even have to give them a bath anymore," she says. "I spray it on, buff them with a towel, and the stink is gone."

Beat them to it. It's not a glamorous job, but some people have resigned themselves to doing a treasure hunt every few days, looking for things in the yard that their dogs are likely to be attracted to, such as dead mice, deer droppings, and rotten bird eggs. They won't smell good when you pick them up, but at least you won't have to live with the smell for 2 weeks because it's permeated your dog's coat all the way down to the skin.

Give them something better. It isn't easy to convince dogs to ignore their natural urge to roll, but food is always a reliable distraction. "Load your pockets with goodies when you're going for a walk," Dr. McConnell says. "But it's going to take a pretty good bribe."

From a dog's point of view, a smelly mud puddle is great fun to play in—especially when there's a friend to share it with.

PUPPY DOG TALES

The Dog Who Lived for Grunge

Rosie is a Labrador–shepherd mix and, according to her owner, she's the sweetest dog there ever was. Sweet, that is, in terms of her disposition. Rosie's personal aroma, on the other hand, is anything but floral.

"Rosie is a roll-aholic," says Maria Stone, Rosie's owner. "We'll be walking down the sidewalk, and all of sudden she'll be squirming around on her back, trying to get as much of whatever she found onto her hide as she possibly can."

At one time, Rosie lived in rural New Mexico, where she had plenty of opportunities to indulge. "There were pig farms and dairy farms in the neighborhood—more animal crud than she knew what to do with," Maria says. "There were days when Rosie would come in and it was like a whole barnyard had walked through the living room."

Rosie had her rolling apotheosis about the time she reached her 10th birthday. "We were out running, and when I looked over, Rosie wasn't beside me anymore," Maria says. "I ran back, but I wasn't quick enough."

Rosie, she discovered, had found something very old, very smelly, and very dead. And there she was, writhing around, making happy-sounding grunts, and trying to get it all the way down to her pores.

It took 2 weeks, three bottles of dog shampoo, and a couple of gallons of tomato juice to make Rosie reasonably presentable. But after that day, Maria says, she really never smelled sweet again.

CHAPTER TWELVE

LYING ON THEIR BACKS

Good Feelings, Cool Air

Ellen Carpenter was afraid she was going to have to deliver some tragic news to her daughter-in-law, Susan Carpenter of Glocester, Rhode Island. As Ellen stood in the kitchen looking out the window, she noticed that the family's much-loved Samoyed, Buddy, was on the lawn, flat on his back with his legs sticking in the air. The first thought that jumped into her mind was that Buddy had been poisoned. She tapped on the window. Buddy didn't budge. She banged loudly on the glass. There was no response. With tears in her eyes, she walked outside, knelt beside Buddy, and reached out to stroke his stomach.

Buddy rolled his eyes open, licked his chops in gratitude for the belly rub, yawned widely, and went back to sleep.

More than a few people have experienced similar moments of panic. Many animals do go belly-up when they expire. Dogs, however, lie on their backs for the sheer pleasure of it, especially when they're getting ready to take a nap. It's a position that indicates that they're pretty darn happy with life.

"A dog who sleeps on his back is a dog who's really comfortable and who feels very safe," says Cynthia Jacobs, D.V.M., a veterinarian in Clarksville, Arkansas.

It's hard to overestimate the sense of personal security that inspires dogs to assume this position. The belly is their softest, most vulnerable part. Dogs are naturally inclined to keep it protected and out of sight. The only times they lie on their backs are when they're trying to appease another dog (or a person) by showing how helpless they are or when they're feeling so safe and peaceful that they forget all about their instinctive trepidation.

Dogs often lie on their backs as a means of temperature control. The sparse fur on their bellies allows the breeze to reach their skin more easily and cool them off.

This shih tzu mix has it all figured out: a comfortable position on his back, his owner's attention, and the chance of a belly rub, as well.

Feels Good to Me

Once dogs are sufficiently secure to lie on their backs—and in today's pet-loving families, it usually doesn't take very long—they find all kinds of good reasons to do it, says Dr. Jacobs. In hot weather, for example, dogs often lie on their backs as a form of climate control. "They curl up to keep warm and stretch out to cool off," she says. Dogs have less hair and more nerve endings on their bellies than on their backs, so exposing their bellies to the air probably feels very good.

Getting the sun is another reason dogs lie on their backs. Apart from their noses, the belly is the only place that isn't covered with thick fur. Dogs don't think about sunburn, and the sensation of direct sunlight is pleasant. "My dog suns herself by lying on her back and holding a stick in her mouth," says Dr. Jacobs. "You'd think she was in heaven."

Finally, many dogs lie on their backs simply because they know it gets them noticed. When they have reason to believe that a belly rub is on the way, or they hope to invite one, they'll roll over, splay their legs apart, and put their bellies in the most "petable" position. "When your dog rolls over on his back in front of you, he's usually asking for your love and attention," says Jeff Nichol, D.V.M., a veterinarian in Albuquerque, New Mexico. "If he gets a belly rub by doing it, you can bet he's going to be smart enough to do it again soon."

"Bang, You're Dead"

Digger is a 6-year-old terrier mix who has transformed a comfortable body position into performance art. When he was a puppy, he learned to play cops and robbers. The game was simple. Someone would say, "Bang," and Digger would roll over on his back.

It didn't take Digger long to perfect his routine, says Sandy Fitzsimmons of San Jose, California. His stage managers—Sandy's three young girls—were less professional, however. They got so excited by the game that they praised Digger even before the "bang-roll-over" sequence was completed.

As a result, Digger began to jump the gun. Now, rather than waiting for "bang," he keels over as soon as he thinks someone's going to say it. "I have to tell him, 'No, Digger, not yet,'" Sandy says. "He gets all excited and flips over on his back as soon as I point my finger."

Now That You Understand...

Take the hint. A dog who's lying on his back should look happy and relaxed. If his sides are heaving and his tongue's hanging out, he's probably too hot for comfort and is trying to catch a breeze, says Vint Virga, D.V.M., a veterinarian at the College of Veterinary Medicine at Cornell University in Ithaca, New York. It's not the best form of air-conditioning, however. Most dogs prefer to lie belly-down on a cool surface when they're hot. One way to help them get more comfortable is to hose down a shady area in the yard where they can lie down and cool off. Indoors, encourage your dog to make himself at home in the kitchen, bathroom, or another area that has tile or wood floors, which are much cooler than carpet.

Use sunscreen. Dogs who spend a lot of time lounging on their backs in the sun sometimes get sunburned. Veterinarians recommend applying a sunscreen with an SPF of 15 or higher. It's fine to use human sunscreens as long as they don't contain zinc oxide or PABA, which can be harmful should dogs lick them off.

If your dog is already sunburned, you can apply an over-the-counter anesthetic spray, such as Solarcaine or Lanacane. Anesthetic ointments are helpful, too. It's worth taking care of the irritation because, otherwise, dogs will scratch the area, which may get infected.

Stop the snores. The one problem with dogs who sleep on their backs is that this position can make them prodigious snorers, says Dr. Jacobs. Don't lie awake yourself because your dog looks so cozy that you hate to disturb him. Give him a nudge, she advises. He'll roll over on his side, and that will quiet the snores.

Give him what he wants. Belly rubs are one of the best opportunities people get to bond with pets, says Dr. Nichol. "Dogs don't initiate many of their interactions with their owners," he explains. "Here's one situation where your dog actually gets to ask for what he wants and receive it from you."

Rubbing your dog's belly does more than make him feel great, Dr. Nichol adds. It's also an effective way to remind him of your parental authority. "Because lying on their backs is such a submissive position, every time you give your dog a belly rub, you reinforce your position as the head of the house in the gentlest, most effective way possible."

Dogs instinctively understand that lying on a tiled floor will keep them cooler than settling down on carpet. It's a natural kind of air conditioning.

CHAPTER THIRTEEN

GOBBLING FOOD

Like Money in the Bank

Every day at 9:00 A.M., Willoughby gets his 4 cups of dog food, which he scarfs in 3 minutes flat. Despite his obvious excitement and the exuberance of his feed-me dance, his owner, Jane Rudnitsky of Oneonta, New York, can't tell if he takes any joy in the meal itself. She wonders if he even tastes it.

She has good reason to wonder. Dogs only have about 1,500 taste buds (people have 10,000). They really don't care about having delectable food. They'll happily settle for edible. "They're like my 9-year-old, who inhales meals so he can get back to his computer game," says Marty Becker, D.V.M., a veterinarian in Bonners Ferry, Idaho, and coauthor of *Chicken Soup for the Pet Lover's Soul.* "It's almost a mechanical act for them. The nutrients have to go in, but there's not much passion for the taste."

Most dogs find that leftovers in the trash are every bit as wonderful as fresh food in their bowls. Either way, they usually eat as fast as they possibly can. There's a good reason for this. When your main concern is

Dogs who share a bowl feel compelled to eat as much and as quickly as they can, just to keep others from getting to it first.

getting enough to eat—and in millennia past, dogs could never take this for granted—haste counts more than taste. Modern dogs can dilly-dally over their food indefinitely and not have to worry about it disappearing, but their predecessors weren't so lucky. They knew that food not eaten right away wouldn't still be in the woods waiting for them later.

Saving Up for a Rainy Day

Dogs evolved from wolves, and wolves are prodigious eaters. They're capable of consuming as much as 40 pounds of meat in a sitting, says Rolan Tripp, D.V.M., a veterinarian in La Mirada, California, who specializes in animal

Many dogs will steal as much food as they possibly can, so you may have to feed your dogs separately to ensure that they all get enough to eat.

behavior. Ancient dogs and their wolfish ancestors didn't stuff themselves just to be pigs. They were hunters and they had to catch their own meat. They didn't have the luxury of knowing where the next meal was coming from. Maybe Monday would bring a deer, but Tuesday might yield a rabbit or a squirrel or, in many cases, nothing at all. Dogs could easily go for several days without a meal, but only if they were well-fed the rest of the time. They knew enough to fill up when they got the chance.

And speed was important. Dogs used to live in packs, tight-knit groups who depended on teamwork to survive. They hunted together and,

when they were successful, shared one big meal at the end of the day. But their idea of sharing wasn't the same as ours. Dogs in packs weren't all equal. There were high-ranking dogs, low-ranking dogs, and dogs in between. They ate in order of their ranks in the pack. The leaders ate first and got the choicest bits, while lower-ranking dogs cleaned up the leftovers. It wasn't easy for every dog to get his fill. So they naturally ate as fast and as much as they could, when they could. Dogs have only been living with humans for about 10,000 years, and old evolutionary habits hang on. Dogs today don't have to hunt, and they get more or less the same amounts of food at the same times. But they still have remnants of the urge to fill up fast just in case their food gets taken away. And they eat even faster when there are other dogs in the family. More dogs mean more competition. Whether or not there's a threat to their food, they don't want to take any chances. So they gobble as fast and furiously as they can.

The Price of Gluttony

The passion that dogs put into eating can be a little off-putting to the people who feed them—and who have to watch their terrible manners. There's the drooling and whining. The unseemly snorting as they bury their faces in their food. And, worst of all, the regurgitation that may occur afterward. This, too, is part of nature's plan.

When wolves stuffed themselves with 40 pounds of meat, their bodies couldn't actually process that much at once. So they would waddle away from the table, throw up a little bit, then eat it to get the nutrients.

Dogs are a lot smaller than wolves, and it doesn't take 40 pounds of meat to turn their stomachs. That's why the kibble you pour in the bowl occasionally gets deposited in the corner a few minutes later. This has nothing to do with physical health or social graces. Their brains and stomachs are telling them that dogs who waste not, want not, and so they follow orders.

Now That You Understand...

Given a chance to raid the food bag, most dogs will instantly revert to their old habits. Even when they don't eat a lot, they do eat fast, and eating fast means that what goes in is going to try to come out. Here are a few ways to protect the floors and keep their stomachs calm.

Give them more time. Dogs learn from experience. If you always pick up the food bowl the minute they're done, they'll figure that they'd better eat faster just in case you pick it up early. Leaving the bowl on the floor for 10 to 15 minutes after it's empty will help them understand that they don't have to rush, says Dr. Becker.

Wet the food. Most dogs like a little gravy with their meals, and moistening dry food with warm water makes it more appealing. More important, it makes it easier to digest, says Dr. Becker. Dogs are less likely to toss up their food when it's not in hard chunks, he explains.

Give them less food, more often. Even though dogs are designed to handle very large meals, it's better for their digestion to eat smaller amounts, more often, says Dr. Tripp. Veterinarians often recommend feeding dogs at least twice a day. Some say it's better to feed them three, four, or even five times a day. The total amount of food will be the same, but the leisurely pace will help ensure that it stays where it's supposed to.

FAST FIX Putting a large object in the middle of your dog's food bowl will force him to coax out each bite. This means he'll have to eat more slowly, says Dr. Becker. It doesn't matter what you put in the bowl, as long as it's not appetizing and it's big enough that it won't get swallowed accidentally. A large butternut squash works well. For small dogs, a tennis ball is fine as long as they don't show more interest in the ball than in their food.

PART TWO

"I Know Things That You Don't"

The Amazing Senses of Dogs

Dogs see the world in ways that we can hardly imagine. Their senses of smell and hearing are vastly better than ours, while their vision leaves something to be desired. When they act in ways that seem unusual to us, they're often responding to something of which only they are aware.

BARKING AT BUTTERFLIES

They're Very Tempting Targets

ebra Doyle lives in Walls, Mississippi, and her dog, a Chow Chow named Bear, is perfectly suited for rural life. Bear likes looking out the window and watching the world go by. He gets especially excited when butterflies pass. There's something about their slow, fluttery, unpredictable movements that make him stand up and bark ... and bark.

Bear's hardly the only dog who gets excited by butterflies. "Dogs are hardwired hunters, so they want to chase after anything that passes by," says Katherine Houpt, V.M.D., Ph.D., a diplomate of the American College of Veterinary Behaviorists and a professor in the College of Veterinary Medicine at Cornell University in Ithaca, New York.

Dogs who are truly hunting, however, don't bark much because that would alert their prey, she adds. In Bear's case, the "prey" is on one side of the glass, and he's on the other. There's something out there he wants to chase, but he can't get at it. He barks out of frustration. Even if the window weren't there, he'd still bark because the odds of catching a butterfly aren't very good. If he really thought he had a chance for success, he'd be very quiet, Dr. Houpt explains.

One reason dogs get so excited—and frustrated—by butterflies is that butterflies seem as though they'd be easy to catch. They're big, they flutter close to the ground, and they don't move very fast. So dogs keep trying, and nearly every time the butterflies stay just out of reach. It drives dogs crazy because no matter how often they fail, the urge to chase is extremely strong, says Mark Plonsky, Ph.D., a dog trainer and professor

Dogs look out windows for the same reason people do—to see if anything interesting is happening. A passing butterfly can bring on a barking frenzy.

Why do dogs eat flies?

Dogs dislike insects. They don't like the sensation of prickly insect feet crawling on them, and the buzzing of flies probably irritates them as much as it does us. Combine this antipathy with their natural hunting instincts, and it's easy to see why they often go snapping at flies, then swallow them when they succeed in catching them.

"When you watch dogs going after flies, you'll see that they stalk them like prey, and they seem to get real joy out of catching one," says Kay Cox, Ph.D., an animal-behavior consultant in Gilbert, Arizona. They're probably indifferent to the taste, she adds. "You don't see dogs chewing and savoring their flies," she says. "Instead, what you see is the 'Aha!' satisfaction of having caught them."

of psychology at the University of Wisconsin at Stevens Point.

"That pull is almost magnetic," he says. When a dog can't keep up with the creature that's taunting him, he has to do something. That may mean barking. Or running in circles. Some dogs will open their mouths and let loose with a whole series of yawns—the canine equivalent of taking a big breath and counting to 10.

Something to Talk About

Apart from giving voice to their hunting instincts, dogs bark at butterflies as a way of being social. These are usually the same dogs who bark when they hear or see something out of the ordinary. They know that something is happening, and they want to share the news.

"Some dogs are just naturally more inclined to be verbal than others," says Kay Cox, Ph.D., an animal-behavior consultant in Gilbert, Arizona. "It can be any dog, but beagles, terriers, and poodles are the ones who seem to do it the most. They want to tell you about everything."

It's not necessarily the butterflies themselves that get these dogs so excited, Dr. Cox adds. It goes back to their breeding. They were bred to bark as a way of communicating with hunters. "They were supposed to bark to scare up quarry, to tell the hunter when they had it in the tree, and so on. But they don't have any work-related use for that communicative ability anymore, so they find an outlet for it on their own," she says.

Even dogs whose ancestors never hunted will often bark at butterflies as a way of guarding their territory. It's hard to imagine that any dog would think of a butterfly as posing much of a threat, but they react that way to pretty much anything that comes into their space. The butterflies unknowingly contribute to the habit because, sooner or later, they fly away. "When a dog barks and barks at something, and it goes away, he invariably thinks he did it," says Dr. Houpt. A dog

Anything that moves is going to attract a dog's attention, and a large, bobbing balloon is the perfect target for a leap and a snap.

who has conquered one butterfly will feel very happy. He'll want to repeat the satisfying experience—with bigger and louder barks—every chance he gets.

Now That You Understand...

Keep your voice low. No one enjoys listening to round after round of senseless barking. After a while, nearly everyone responds with a loud bark—"Quiet!"—of their own, which only makes their dogs bark more.

"When your dog barks and you yell, he really thinks you're barking with him," says Dr. Cox. "And so he'll bark even louder."

Since dogs use their barks as a way of communicating with others in the family, it's often enough to let them know you've gotten the message. Keeping your voice low and quiet, acknowledge what your dog has seen. Tell him "butterfly," advises Dr. Cox, and follow that with a low-key "quiet." Just as quietly, lead him somewhere where he can't see outside. He'll know you've heard what he has to say, and that will be enough for him, she explains.

FAST FIX Since dogs who are in the house can't hear butterflies outside, you can stop the barking just by closing the blinds, says Dr. Cox. You can also use the blinds as part of a training exercise. After you tell your dog "quiet," shut the blinds. He'll get quiet right away. After a few seconds, open the blinds again. With a little practice, he'll learn that barking less lets him have what he loves—the view out the window—while noisy barking always gets the blinds closed, she says.

Bribe him for quiet. When your dog barks at butterflies and keeps barking until you notice him, try ignoring him the next time. Let him bark as long as he likes. In the meantime, go get a dog treat and go about your business. As soon as your dog stops barking on his own, give him the treat and tell him "good quiet," says Dr. Cox. Some dogs will start barking less after just a few rewards, and nearly all dogs will get quieter within a few weeks of practice.

Dogs will spend hours stalking and snapping at flies, but they hardly ever manage to catch one.

CHAPTER FIFTEEN

EATING DUNG

Following the Crowd

Mother dogs do whatever they have to do to take care of their young. One of their duties is to lick the pups' genitals and bottoms in order to jump-start their ability to urinate and have bowel movements. Another motherly duty is to keep the nest clean. So after revving up their puppies' insides, they eat what comes out.

Dogs have only a fraction of the tastebuds that humans do, so this unpleasant duty doesn't faze them. And from their point of view, it has to be done. Apart from the need for basic housekeeping, eating the puppies' stools once kept dog families alive. Dung has a powerful scent, and it would have advertised the presence of puppies to every hungry predator within sniffing distance, explains Jo Ann Eurell, D.V.M., a veterinarian and animal-behavior specialist at the University of Illinois College of Veterinary Medicine at Urbana-Champaign.

Dogs aren't the only animals who eat the stools of their young. Horses, cats, and many other mammals do it too. But there's a difference. Most

Mother dogs often eat the stools of their puppies to keep the nest clean and to remove any odors that may lead predators to the litter.

animals take care of their young, then never eat dung again. Dogs, on the other hand, sometimes get a taste for it. They keep going after it every chance they get.

He Did It First

Dogs have always lived in groups. First, they lived with other dogs. Now, they live with people. As with all highly social animals, including humans, they're very impressionable. They learn how to play by watching other dogs play. They

Puppies often imitate what older dogs do. There are times when that includes imitating their least desirable behavior—eating dung.

dogs hated the taste of dung, they wouldn't keep eating it. But they do. So there has to be something about it that they like.

This isn't all that surprising. Dogs have always been scavengers, Dr. Eurell explains. They'll eat roadkill as readily as their suppers. Old trash, pond muck, and dead sparrows on the lawn are no less appetizing. Dogs start getting hungry whenever they sniff something with a pungent smell, and dung certainly does smell.

Not all dung tastes the same, of course. Dogs seem to have different preferences. Some are attracted to the stools of deer, cows, or horses. Others will eat the stools of other dogs. And a great many dogs are attracted to cat droppings, possibly because cat foods are very high in protein and the dogs are going after undigested nutrients.

Look at Me

Dogs, no less than children, crave attention. And they do whatever it takes to get it, including things they know you hate. This probably explains why some dogs only eat dung when their owners are around to watch, says Dr. Eurell. It's

learn proper etiquette by following the examples of their elders. And they often eat dung for no other reason than they saw another dog doing it, says Dr. Eurell.

One reason that this habit is so common is that every dog watched his mother do it. Most puppies sample dung at some time or other. But most of them seem to give it up.

Doesn't Taste Bad

Children will often do crazy things because they saw their friends do them first. But once is usually enough. They won't jump out of a tree or put their fingers in a candle flame after the first painful experience. Dogs, however, will return to dung again and again.

Most experts have had to conclude that there's more at work than simple imitation. If

probably the equivalent of a 6-year-old saying a dirty word and then watching for his parents' reaction. "Look at me," the dog is saying.

Boredom has something to do with it too. Dogs entertain themselves by putting things in their mouths. When not much is happening, they often nose around the yard, picking up sticks and putting them down, even mouthing rocks on occasion. Since they aren't offended by the smell or taste of dung, it's just another thing for them to pick up, play with, and explore.

Now That You Understand...

Dogs occasionally eat so much dung that they get sick to their stomachs. For the most part, however, it's not likely to make them sick—although they may get worms from eating the stools of an infected animal. "Their digestive tracts are very forgiving," says Robin Downing, D.V.M., a veterinarian in Windsor, Colorado.

The people who live with dogs, however, are less forgiving. For one thing, it's an ugly sight that no one wants to watch. There's also the fact that dogs who eat dung have heart-stopping bad breath. "It takes some serious devotion to get past that," says Dr. Downing.

FAST FIX Veterinarians sometimes recommend adding garlic, canned pumpkin, or Accent meat tenderizer to a dung-eating dog's food. Assuming that it's his own dung that he's attracted do, these ingredients may give it a taste he dislikes—although it's hard to imagine that anything could make it taste worse than it already does. This isn't a perfect solution, but it does work for some dogs, says Dr. Eurell. A product called For-bid, available in pet supply stores, does the same thing and may help, she adds.

Add some seasoning. People won't eat food with too much salt, and dogs won't eat dung that has been sprinkled with ground red pepper. Taking a few minutes each day to season the stuff your dog usually eats—in the litter box, for example—will make it less appetizing. Even if your dog does take a bite, he'll wonder what the heck he's gotten into.

This isn't something that you can do halfway, however. If you do it for just a day or two, your dog will be resourceful enough to sniff out something that hasn't been treated. The idea is to treat the dung long enough that he assumes it's always going to taste like that. And once he gives it up for a while, he may forget all about it, says Dr. Eurell.

Switch to a concentrated food. Average dog foods are designed for the average dog. They have an abundance of nutrients, but some dogs simply need more than these foods provide. They may turn to dung as a way of supplementing their diets. It's worth switching to a premium dog food, says Dr. Downing. These foods provide highly concentrated nutrition in a form that's easy for dogs to digest. If their bodies' needs are being met, they may be less likely to look for extras, she explains.

Feeding your dog two or three times a day may help, too. Dogs who eat only once a day get hungry between meals. Feeding them more often will keep their stomachs satisfied, and they'll be less likely to forage on their own, says Dr. Downing.

CHAPTER SIXTEEN

ATTRACTED TO VERTICAL OBJECTS

It's Where the Big Dogs Go

When people and dogs go for walks, it's almost as though they're on completely different trips. "I see all the same things I saw the day before—the same trees, the same mailboxes, the same fire hydrants," says Mark Plonsky, Ph.D., a dog trainer and professor of psychology at the University of Wisconsin at Stevens Point. His dog, however, is "seeing" with his nose. The scents he encounters are changing all the time.

A tree by the sidewalk, for example, contains hundreds of scents humans don't know exist. But dogs recognize them as clearly as we see the branches and the leaves. They're especially attuned to the smells of other dogs. A quick sniff tells them who's been there before them, how big and dominant they were, whether they were male or female, even if they were in good health. "That tree might as well be a signed guest book," says Dr. Plonsky.

The reason vertical objects such as telephone poles and fire hydrants have so much appeal is that they provide a canvas for dogs to project their social aspirations. In their world, size makes a difference. Bigger dogs can "claim" more territory than smaller ones. "The thinking seems to be, 'The higher I urinate, the bigger other dogs will think I am,'" say Emily Weiss, curator of behavior and research at the Sedgwick County Zoo in Wichita, Kansas. Some dogs go so far as to choose the highest tree on a hill, and then try to mark the highest spot on that tree.

Some dogs are so determined to get their marks up high that they get downright athletic. Some raise their legs over their heads in order to

An essential part of this golden retriever's routine is checking out who's been visiting his district. It makes his daily patrol around his territory more interesting.

If sniffing starts at the front gate and continues at every fence post until you arrive home, it makes for a very long walk. Dogs who are leash-trained are easier to manage—and to keep moving.

tend to be the most dominant, and dominant dogs are more attractive to the opposite sex. For males, hitting a high spot on a tree is an opportunity to announce their availability as well as their status, Weiss says. For females, sniffing the different levels gives them a variety of mates to choose from.

The messages contained in a droplet of urine—and a dog's ability to detect them—are hard for humans to imagine. Dogs have nearly 20 square inches of scent-detecting membrane. Humans only have $1/2$ square inch. In addition, dogs have a small mass of nerve endings in the roof of the mouth called the Jacobson's organ. It responds only to odors linked to food and sex. When a dog sniffs urine markings on a telephone pole, the Jacobson's organ fires off a signal to the hypothalamus, the part of the brain that is responsible for controlling sex drive and appetite.

achieve more upward trajectory, Weiss says. Others back up to trees with their hind ends in the air. Some even stand on their front legs in order to get extra height.

Their efforts don't go unnoticed by other dogs. "Even dogs who don't leave a mark of their own usually want to stop and investigate who's been around," Weiss says. Bragging aside, it's a good way of staying on top of the neighborhood news.

Looking for Love

For dogs who have been neutered, hydrants and other vertical objects are mainly an opportunity to share some gossip—their mating instinct isn't very strong. Dogs who are intact, however, have a very practical reason for aiming high. Big dogs

Now That You Understand...

This fascination with all things upright wouldn't be an issue if dogs took themselves for walks. But there's usually a human at the other end of the leash. A walk around the block can take an impressively long time as dogs do their sniff-and-mark routines. While dogs do need an opportunity to get their bearings and catch up on the latest gossip—and to leave some of their own—there's no reason it should take all day.

Dogs who are leash-trained know that they're not supposed to stop until their owners give them the go-ahead. If your dog hasn't had basic obedience, you're going to have to teach him to heel. And the only way he'll learn that is by watching you all the time to see when you want him to stay close or when it's okay to take a break. "When he's keeping his eyes on you, he won't be wandering off exploring new smells," Dr. Plonsky adds.

He has developed an unusual technique for teaching dogs to watch him. "I spit food at them," he explains. During the early stages of training, Dr. Plonsky puts tiny pieces of cooked hot dog in his mouth, one at a time. Periodically, he'll pop one out so the dogs can get it. "Once they've done it a few times, they learn not to take their eyes off my face," he says.

Keeping a dog focused on you is one way of stopping him from investigating every tree he passes. This Border collie is intent on the ball in his owner's hand.

The Smell of Boy

Most dogs spend their free time sniffing fire hydrants and tree trunks. But some use their talented schnozzles for a higher purpose, as a bloodhound named Mac proved one day when a neighborhood child wandered away from home. No one had a clue where he was, and his parents were afraid that he might have gotten lost in the nearby forest.

The police, after a preliminary (and unsuccessful) search, called Mac's owner, Captain Paula Wyatt of the Hopewell Sheriff's Department in Virginia. Mac is trained in search-and-rescue, but even so, the situation didn't look good, Paula remembers. The boy had been gone for more than 12 hours—more than enough time for his scent to have faded. Worse, the police, neighbors, and other dogs had already been searching for hours, covering the boy's scent with their own.

Paula asked for something belonging to the boy. Someone gave her a pillowcase. She held it out, and Mac sniffed it thoroughly. Then Paula snapped on his harness, and they started the search. Everyone stood back and watched as the excited bloodhound went to work. He aimed right for the woods. He crisscrossed his own tracks, followed a stream, stuck his nose in the water now and then, and took detour after detour. It seemed like he was going in circles—but then, that's how a lot of children get around. Mac knew what he was doing.

In the end, after searching for almost 2 hours, Mac ran right up to the boy, who was sitting on a log in the nearby woods. He greeted the boy by licking him from head to toe.

50

CHAPTER SEVENTEEN

COCKING THEIR HEADS
A Way of Capturing Sound

It wasn't by accident that advertising for RCA once featured a dog cocking his head in front of a speaker horn. There's something about this position that most people find utterly adorable. Dogs know it, too—which is why they do it, even when they aren't trying to hear anything in particular.

"We give them a positive response, and they remember that," says Emily Weiss, curator of behavior and research at Sedgwick County Zoo in Wichita, Kansas.

The Better to Hear You

Dogs don't start off cocking their heads to get human approval, of course. They do it for a very practical reason. Tilting the head to the side puts one of the ears up and forward. By turning an ear in the direction of fuzzy or inaudible sounds, dogs are able to hear a little more clearly, explains Rolan Tripp, D.V.M., a veterinarian in La Mirada, California, who specializes in animal behavior.

We often forget how confusing human speech is for dogs. Even though dogs understand some of what we're saying, most of our conversation is just a blur of sound to them. Usually, they just ignore it. They can tell from our body language and eye movements when we're saying things that concern them. Once something attracts their interest, they'll often perk up their ears and tilt their heads slightly in order to figure out what's going on, Weiss says.

Dogs rarely cock their heads when sounds are coming from the sides, since their ears are already in prime hearing position. They mainly do it when people are in front of them, since the sound waves aren't traveling directly toward the ears, explains Weiss.

You'll see this more in puppies than older dogs, adds Dr. Tripp. It's not that puppies have more trouble hearing. They just haven't been around us long enough to figure out what's important and what isn't. So they respond to almost any sound with a little head-cock, especially when we're looking at them at the same time. They know something interesting is happening, and they don't want to miss a thing.

Human speech is confusing for dogs. They often cock their heads to make sense out of the babble of noise. The movement allows them to capture every bit of sound.

When dogs are trying to pinpoint the source of a sound, they'll cock their heads to bring things into clearer focus.

When dogs cock their heads, gravity pulls one of the earflaps away from the auditory canal. Essentially, this opens the "cup" and allows more sound to flow in, says Dr. Tripp. This may be particularly important for Lhasa apsos, Maltese, and Pekingese, who tend to have a lot of hair in their ears. "If you put a little cotton in your ear, loosely covered it with a hat, and tried to hear, you'd have pretty much the same effect," he says.

Head cocking also helps dogs see a little better. Unlike people, who generally see things more clearly the closer they are, dogs don't see well at all when things are less than a few feet way, says Christopher J. Murphy, D.V.M., Ph.D., professor of ophthalmology at the School of Veterinary Medicine at the University of Wisconsin at Madison. When you're right next to your dog and he's cocking his head, he may be trying to bring you into focus, he explains.

Now That You Understand...

Dogs hear a lot better than people do, partly because their ears are incredibly mobile. They have 15 different muscles that can move the ears in all directions. This helps them detect and understand sounds no matter where they're coming from. Head cocking is just another tool they use to hear clearly. Dogs shouldn't be doing it all the time, however. When they are, they may need some extra help to hear.

Speak in a higher voice. One way dogs decide what's worth listening to and what isn't

Natural Limitations

The way a dog's ears are designed may play some role in how much he cocks his head. Pricked-up ears may be slightly more efficient than other ear shapes, since sound waves are able to go right in. Floppy ears present a problem. The sound waves have to pass through a big, heavy earflap before reaching the eardrum. This probably doesn't make a big difference, but dogs with heavy, hanging ears may have to work a little harder in order to hear what's being said, says Dr. Tripp.

"The inside of a dog's ear is shaped like a cup," Weiss adds. This design allows the ears to scoop in sound waves—but only when the opening is unencumbered.

CALL FOR HELP

Even though it's normal for dogs to cock their heads in order to hear (and see) better, they shouldn't be doing it too often. A dog whose head seems to be in perpetual tilt mode probably has an ear problem that isn't going to get better on its own, says Rolan Tripp, D.V.M., a veterinarian in La Mirada, California, who specializes in animal behavior.

A damaged eardrum or an inner-ear infection can make it hard for dogs to hear, he explains. In some cases, ear problems can throw off a dog's internal sense of balance, which will also cause him to tilt his head. "Any time a dog carries his head tilted for more than a few minutes, he needs to visit his veterinarian," says Dr. Tripp.

Dogs with ear infections often shake their heads as well as tilt them, Dr. Tripp adds. Use a flashlight to light the inside of your dog's ear. If you see redness or a discharge, or if you smell an unpleasant odor, he probably has an infection and is going to need antibiotics to knock it out.

Stand where he can see you. Even though a substantial portion of a dog's brain is devoted to sound, a dog always uses his other senses to augment what he's hearing. Standing in front of your dog will allow him to watch your face, eyes, posture, and body movements while you talk, explains Dr. McConnell. Even if your dog isn't hearing clearly, he'll be able to gather a lot of information from your body language about what you're trying to tell him.

Trim the ears. Dogs with unusually hairy ears may hear a little better if you remove some of the fluff, says Dr. Tripp. You can use blunt-ended scissors to trim some hair from the outer part of the earflaps, but groomers usually prefer plucking. Dogs don't enjoy having their ears plucked and will often put up a fight, so you may want to pay a groomer to do it for you.

Dogs who tilt or shake their heads constantly may have an ear infection. Use a flashlight to check for redness or discharge. If the ear looks irritated, you need to see a vet.

is by the sound frequency. High-pitched sounds get their attention, probably because they resemble the sounds made by traditional prey such as rabbits and chipmunks. Pitching your voice upward will get your dog's attention and let him know that he needs to listen carefully to what you're about to say, explains Patricia McConnell, Ph.D., a certified applied animal behaviorist in Black Earth, Wisconsin.

CHAPTER EIGHTEEN

HANGING THEIR HEADS OUT CAR WINDOWS

They Smell Things We Don't

People need to get over the idea that all things intelligent belong exclusively to humans. Our dogs undoubtedly consider us to be handicapped, nearly disabled, by our astonishingly poor sense of smell. Experts estimate that dogs can catch a whiff of something that's one million times less concentrated than what humans can detect. With so much sniff power, it's hardly surprising that they stick their heads out car windows. They could care less about the scenery. What they're after are smells.

"If you're driving through town at 30 miles an hour and your dog has his nose out the window, he knows where the bakery is, where the butcher shop is, which street leads to the local McDonald's, and maybe even what the mayor had for breakfast," says Myrna Milani, D.V.M., a veterinarian in Claremont, New Hampshire, and author of *DogSmart.*

More Speed, Better Smells

Dogs assume a characteristic expression when they put their faces into the wind: Their upper lips curl, their noses wrinkle, their eyes partly close, and their ears fold back. It looks as though they're experiencing a moment of ecstasy—which they probably are—but mainly they're concentrating. "It's as though they're closing down all the rest of their senses to focus on this one," says Dr. Milani.

There's a world of fascinating scents outside the car. This mixed-breed dog loves to hang her head out the window and sample every one of them.

All dogs, from huge Great Danes to tiny terriers, have extraordinarily acute senses of smell. Their scenting ability is enhanced when they are moving quickly, which is one reason that they take advantage of open car windows.

Smells are so important to dogs that they have two separate systems for detecting them. One is the nose system. It consists of a huge amount of tissue called olfactory epithelium, which is loaded with scent receptors. This area takes up about $1/2$ square inch in humans, but up to 20 square inches in some dog breeds. As air moves over the tissue, odor molecules settle in millions of scent receptors. The more air flow there is, the more scents dogs detect.

"Dogs' sense of smell is enhanced when they're moving quickly," adds Vint Virga, D.V.M., a veterinarian at the College of Veterinary Medicine at Cornell University in Ithaca, New York. In the evolutionary scheme of things, this probably made them better hunters because they could load up on scents while chasing prey.

Dogs have a second smelling system that's headquartered in their mouths. Near the upper incisors is a tiny duct that leads to a specialized gland called Jacobson's organ. It's designed to capture and interpret the most primitive types of smells. Dogs depend on it to identify other dogs, choose a mate, and smell prey. When dogs scrunch up their faces in the wind, it looks like they're catching flies, but what they're really doing is catching scents, says Dr. Milani.

PUPPY DOG TALES

The Road Hound

Riding a motorcycle requires proper balance and a low center of gravity, neither of which dogs have in abundance. This is regrettable because riding in the open air is their favorite way to sniff the breeze. Jon and Vicki Marsh of Frankfort, Indiana, found a way to overcome nature's limitations and allow their Rottweiler mix, Indy, to experience life on the road. He rides in a sidecar attached to their Honda Gold Wing, with his nose pushed forward and goggles securely covering his eyes.

Indy started riding motorcycles when he was 6 months old, and it has become his favorite pastime. In some ways, he's a better passenger than people are, Jon adds. Indy doesn't shift around too much, which helps the motorcycle stay balanced.

Riding a motorcycle isn't without risks, of course. The main problem is other drivers who can't believe what they're seeing, Jon says. They slow down at first, then speed up and get as close as they can to make sure their eyes aren't playing tricks on them—that what they're seeing really is a robust Rottweiler riding a little to the right of center, with his ears blown back and a very happy look on his face.

BREED SPECIFIC

Dogs don't see very well, so they're usually indifferent to passing scenery. Dogs called sighthounds, however, depend on their eyes more than on their noses. For Afghans, salukis, and greyhounds, riding in a car provides a visual as well as an emotional thrill.

These dogs are attracted to things that run—and when they're in a speeding car, everything outside looks like it's running. Wide-open windows aren't recommended for sighthounds because when they see something "running," they tend to do what nature intended—dive after it and commence the chase.

Now That You Understand...

Veterinarians are always telling people not to let their dogs put their heads out the windows because a ladybug doing 65 miles an hour can do serious damage. But people do it anyway because their dogs love it and it's hard to resist. Rather than having to make a choice between safety and canine satisfaction, here are a few compromises you may want to try.

Strain the air. Now you can do for cars what you've always done with windows at home—put up screens. Products called window vent guards are designed to fit into any car window. You can put them in and take them out in seconds, and they fold small enough to fit in the glove box, says Dr. Milani. The screens don't interfere with scent-laden air. Your dog will still catch a good breeze, but without the risk of catching debris in the face. The guards are available from pet supply stores and catalogs.

Give an inch. Open windows wouldn't be so dangerous if dogs were satisfied to sit in the backseat and breathe deeply. But from their point of view, nothing beats climbing halfway outside—and every year, a few dogs lean too far and actually fall out, says Dr. Milani. She recommends opening the window far enough so that your dog can put out his nose, but not so far that he'll stick out his whole head. He'll still get the sensory rush, but without the risk.

Lock him in place. Seat belts are a good idea even if your dog doesn't see open windows as an invitation to freedom. Pet supply manufacturers have developed a variety of safety harnesses that are designed to lock into existing seat belts. Buckling dogs in their seats keeps them from roaming, protects them in the event of an accident, and puts them in a prime position to catch the wind without having to poke their heads out the windows.

A window vent guard lets dogs catch scents while keeping debris out of their eyes and noses.

CHAPTER NINETEEN

AFRAID OF THUNDER

A World Turned Upside Down

At any given moment, about 2,000 thunderstorms are raging around the world, with lightning hitting the ground 100 times a second. What this means is that there are more than 2,000 reasons for dogs to dive under the bed, howl at the sky, and claw, chew, or bark their way through the house, looking for comfort from the storm.

"The thing about thunder is that we're not just talking about noise," says Myrna Milani, D.V.M., a veterinarian in Claremont, New Hampshire, and author of *DogSmart*. "There's a whole big scary event that comes along with it."

Dogs' senses are much sharper than ours. They hear, smell, and sense things with a clarity that we can hardly imagine. Because they hear higher and lower frequencies than we do, the sound of thunder is more intense. Their hearing is sensitive, so the volume is much higher. Then there are the changes in atmospheric pressure that accompany storms, and the gusting winds that bring sudden changes in airborne scents.

"With all that, plus lightning, thunder, and rain, a storm is nothing less than a full assault on the senses," says Dr. Milani. "Thunder is one thing most dogs pin their fears on, but it's not the only one. It's just the most obvious and the most disruptive."

In addition, dogs aren't able to understand what's causing all the commotion. You can't tell them that storms are a normal meteorological phenomenon. All they know is that the world has suddenly changed, and it's not a change for the better.

When thunderstorms are raging, a dog's natural instinct is to take cover in an enclosed place, such as under the bed, where he'll feel safer.

A Shocking Night

Linda and Reese Gardiner's dogs aren't afraid of thunder, but they are afraid of fire, and for good reason. One summer night in their home in Davie, Florida, the Gardiners were sleeping soundly in their beds. Both of them are deaf, so the thunder booming outside didn't disturb them. Their two poodles, Peanut and Pepper, were paying very close attention, however.

Peanut and Pepper haven't had formal training as service dogs, but both of them alert the Gardiners to sounds that the people wouldn't otherwise hear. When the phone rings, for example, one or both dogs will let them know. They do the same thing when someone comes to the door at night. Storms don't bother them, but they do listen carefully to what's out there. On this particular night, their vigilance paid off because a falling power line hit the house and ignited the air conditioner.

Both dogs immediately bounded onto the bed and nudged the Gardiners to wake them up. Then they ran to the window, back to the bed, and to the window again, trying to draw the couple's attention. Linda finally got out of bed, looked out the window, and saw the sparks. She quickly shut off the air conditioner, and the sparks died out.

The danger past, Peanut and Pepper both curled up and went to sleep, happy that they'd done a good night's work.

Good Intentions, Bad Results

No one knows why some dogs are terrified of thunder while others are oblivious. The fears tend to be worse in big dogs, which has led some experts to speculate that they may be able to hear low-frequency rumblings that smaller dogs

miss. In addition, breeds who work closely with people, such as Labrador retrievers, suffer most, probably because these dogs feel that it's their job to protect their people, and storms leave them feeling helpless because they can't bark or bite away the danger. "Here's something that they see as a threat and can't do a thing about," says Dr. Milani. "It makes them feel totally out of control."

The way that people react to their dogs' nervousness has a lot to do with how well the dogs cope with storms, adds Betty Fisher, an animal behaviorist and trainer in San Diego and coauthor of *So Your Dog's Not Lassie*. Dogs who are frightened look to their people for reassurance. When the people seem upset—not because of the storm, but because their dogs are obviously terrified—the dogs think something like, "Wow, they're scared too! I guess this really is a problem."

"The best way to handle storms is to pay as little attention to your dog as possible until it's over," Fisher says. "Let him stay near you, but don't baby him. When dogs hear worried tones in our voices—especially the tone that says, 'It's okay, mommy's here'—they become convinced that there's really something to be afraid of."

A similar thing occurs when people try to coax dogs out of their hiding places. All the dogs want is a place to feel safe. They can't understand why people are sticking their heads under the bed and trying to bribe or pull them out. They've never seen people acting that way before, and it freaks them out.

A sleeping bag creates a cozy, den-like space in which dogs can burrow down and ride out the storm in comfort.

Now That You Understand...

Hold them like Mom did. Mother dogs control and reassure their pups by holding them behind their ears or on the bridges of their noses. You can give dogs the same feelings of reassurance by buckling them into special collars such as the Gentle Leader or the Halti. Unlike traditional collars, which go around the neck, these are like harnesses that slip over the nose and behind the ears. They're perfect for dogs who are trembling because of thunder. "It's like behavioral acupressure," says Dr. Milani. "They give your dog the same kind of feeling that a 3-year-old child has when mom or dad is standing behind him and holding him by the shoulder."

Putting dogs on leashes during storms helps too, Fisher adds. Leashes are symbols of parental authority, and dogs will relax when they know that someone else is in charge of things.

Tranquilize them with a sleeping bag. Dogs naturally gravitate to small, enclosed places, which is why they often lie down in the midst of shoes, clothes, or other things on the floor—it's their way of creating a little den. The urge to hide is especially strong when they're frightened. Dr. Milani recommends unzipping a sleeping bag and putting it where your dog usually spends her time. She'll appreciate the comfort, and the thick folds will allow her to burrow in and create a little enclosed space.

Give an herbal sedative. Some of the same natural tranquilizers that work for people also work for dogs. Supplements with ingredients such as melatonin and chamomile, available in pet supply stores and catalogs, can make it much easier for dogs to relax during storms, says Elizabeth Brown, D.V.M., a veterinarian in Sarasota, Florida.

Try a soothing touch. A technique called Tellington Touch, which isn't quite acupressure and is not quite massage, has been shown to help dogs relax. One stroke that seems to ease storm anxiety is the ear touch. Hold the ear between your thumb and forefinger and give gentle strokes, moving from the base to the tip.

CHAPTER TWENTY

LOSING TOYS
BETWEEN THEIR PAWS

Too Close to See

If dogs wore glasses, they'd all have bifocals that were thin at the top and as thick as Coke bottles on the bottom. They can see fairly well at a distance, but reading *The New York Times* is beyond them. Most dogs can't focus at all on objects closer than 1½ feet away. That's why a seemingly smart, highly sensitive dog can lose a rubber cheeseburger that's lying directly under his nose.

The reason for this canine farsightedness lies in their paws: Dogs don't have opposable thumbs the way people do. "They don't need to be able to closely examine things at arm's length," says Christopher J. Murphy, D.V.M., Ph.D., professor of ophthalmology at the School of Veterinary Medicine at the University of Wisconsin at Madison. "As they've evolved, they've needed to be able to catch sight of prey at a distance and keep it in view while they try to run it down." Objects that are just a paw's length away aren't likely to get up and run away, and dogs don't need to see them clearly.

Even if dogs had 20/20 vision, they might not bother looking at things close-up. A large portion of a dog's brain is devoted to processing smells. They depend on smell far more than their other senses, including sight. A dog who is frantically searching for a toy that he knows was right there a minute ago isn't using his eyes very much. All of that head turning and body positioning is an attempt to pull in scent molecules from all directions. It's his sense of smell, not his eyes, that will lead him to the prize. Finding things by smell probably isn't as fast as seeing them clearly, but in the long run, it's just as accurate.

Dog who tend to lose their toys may have less trouble when the toys are large, like this German shepherd's ball. It's also blue, a color that dogs easily see.

A Unique Blind Spot

Blurry vision isn't the only reason dogs lose things that are right in front of them. Unlike people, they have a small (or not so small, depending on the breed) anatomical disadvantage: a very big nose. It's rather like a blind spot in the car—they just can't see around it. The bigger the nose, the bigger the blind spot, says Dr. Murphy.

Once again, this wasn't a disadvantage in the evolutionary scheme of things. Dogs who hunted needed to know what was happening off to the sides and far in front of them. Their eyes are set far apart, which allows them to see an area that encompasses 240 degrees. (Humans, by contrast, can see about 180 degrees.) A tennis ball may disappear when it's right under a dog's nose, but he'll spot it in an instant when it's off to the side.

Dogs see moving things even better, adds Mark Plonsky, Ph.D., a dog trainer and professor of psychology at the University of Wisconsin at Stevens Point. Their eyes are exquisitely sensitive to motion, whether from a rabbit rustling the bushes or a tennis ball rolling across the lawn. Things that are motionless, however, might as well not even be there. Dogs just can't see them as easily.

Now That You Understand...

Since dogs will never have great eyesight—as they get older their vision may get even worse—they can use a little help finding things that, to people, appear to be in plain sight. Rather than

These racing greyhounds can see moving objects extremely well. Once an object stops moving, however, they're much less likely to spot it.

waiting for their noses to kick in, you can make their toys a little more visible.

Pick colors they can see. Dogs don't see colors anywhere near as well as people do. They're essentially color-blind when it comes to distinguishing reds and greens. This can be a problem when, say, they're looking for a green tennis ball on a green lawn. Dr. Plonsky recommends buying toys that are yellow or blue. Dogs can see these colors, and the toys will stand out more clearly against the background.

FAST FIX Dogs who are perpetually losing their toys will have a lot more fun if you simply buy them bigger toys. They're easier to see and keep track of. Your dog will spend less time searching and more time playing, says Dr. Plonsky.

These miniature schnauzers love their hedgehog toy. It's yellow, so it's easy to see. And a small bell inside the toy helps them keep track of it when it's in motion.

Buy toys that make noise. Dogs hear a lot better than people do. In fact, they depend on their sense of hearing almost as much as their sense of smell, says Ralph Hamor, D.V.M., a veterinarian and specialist in ophthalmology at the University of Illinois College of Veterinary Medicine at Urbana. For older dogs especially, balls with little bells inside can be a big help. Even if your dog has trouble seeing the ball, the ringing will lead him to it every time.

Balls with bells don't make noise unless they're moving, of course. So you may want to get a few sets of toys: noisemakers for times when you'll be playing with your dog and larger, brightly colored toys that he'll be able to find when he's playing by himself.

Play in the dark. The eyes contain structures called rods and cones. Rods are responsible for detecting light, and cones for detecting color. As you might expect, people have lots of cones. Dogs have mostly rods. This is why they hardly notice colors but can see better in the dark than we can. So don't stay inside after supper. Take your dog outside and throw his toy for a while. That rubber cheeseburger may be invisible to you after dark, but your dog will find it right away.

Mark toys with scents. The smellier things are, the easier it is for dogs to find them, says Dr. Plonsky. This is especially true when the scents are meaty. Rubbing your dog's ball with a piece of hot dog or wiping it with chicken broth will make it hard to miss. "I can hide my dog's toys in places where there's no way he can see them. But as long as the toys smell, it's as though there's a big neon sign over them," he says. "Dogs' sense of smell is so powerful, it's almost as though they 'see' things with their noses."

BREED SPECIFIC

Labradors and other retrievers usually have very good eyesight. They needed extra sharp vision in order to see and retrieve downed birds. German shepherds and Rottweilers, on the other hand, have a genetic tendency to be short-sighted.

CHAPTER TWENTY-ONE

SNIFFING PRIVATE PLACES

Getting to Know You

People have lots of ways of greeting each other: nods, kisses, handshakes, waves, and high fives, to name just a few. Dogs keep it simple. They sniff each other's bottoms.

Dogs do a lot of things differently from people, and for the most part people are tolerant of these differences, figuring to each species, its own. Not so with rude sniffing. It's obnoxious when dogs do it to people, and it's not much better to stand around while they take their time doing it to each other.

It's not a mystery why dogs sniff each others' privates. Every dog carries ID in his back pocket, so to speak. On each side of the rectum is an anal sac, which contains a strong-smelling fluid. This fluid is the equivalent of a dog's thumbprint, says Char Bebiak, an animal behaviorist and head trainer at the Purina Pet Care Center in Gray Summit, Missouri. With a quick sniff, dogs can tell more about each other than

we could determine by rifling through one another's wallets. "Dogs can tell the sex, age, health, reproductive status, diet, and mood from those smells," says Bebiak. "They get all the information they need to decide whether they want to associate with that dog and what kind of relationship they ought to have."

When dogs meet people, they use the same tried-and-true method that works so well with their peers. It may be uncomfortable and embarrassing for us, but dogs know what they're doing. "Private places offer dogs a lot of information because the scents are more intense than those from other parts of the body," says Robin Kovary, director of the American Dog Trainers Network in New York City. Dogs can pick up as much information about health, hormones, and tension levels from sniffing people as from sniffing other dogs. Research has shown, in fact, that dogs sniff with such accuracy that they may be able to detect some types of cancer or the onset of seizures before people have a clue about the problem.

When dogs meet other dogs, they always give each other a thorough sniffing. Unless they're taught more polite alternatives, they'll take the same approach when they meet people.

Human Interference

A dog who greets people by shoving her nose into their bottoms needs to be taught to stand back and use another, more polite kind of greeting. But you don't want to interrupt dogs when they're doing their usual meet-and-greet with each other. People who tug their dogs away from each other before they've finished their traditional introductions are inadvertently creating social tension, Kovary explains.

The sniffing ritual is designed in part to help dogs establish who has the more forceful personality and deserves extra respect. This is an essential component of all their introductions as well as of the interactions that follow. Interrupting this step by tugging dogs away from each other leaves them uncertain about their respective roles. They may solve this uncertainty by getting physical. So instead of watching a leisurely sniff, you may find yourself in the middle of a fight.

Tugging on the leash in the midst of a dog-to-dog introduction creates another kind of tension as well. Dogs read body language very quickly. When you pull your dog away from another dog, the leash will pull her head upward. This is the position that dogs assume when they're being threatening. So you could inadvertently start a fight by pulling your dog into a position that says, in effect, "And so's your mother."

"Sniffing is the main way dogs sum one another up, and you don't want to make it hard for them to assess a new situation and a new dog," Kovary says.

Now That You Understand...

A nose thrust may be acceptable among dogs, but it's not so pleasant for the two-legged visitors in their lives. Every dog can learn to greet people in more acceptable ways. The secret, Kovary says, is to teach them an alternative to that ancient, secret handshake they know so well.

Start with a shake. The standard greeting among people is the handshake, and dogs can learn it too. Have your dog sit, then stick out your hand, putting it slightly below her nose. Most dogs will instinctively raise a paw to meet it. If your dog doesn't get it and won't raise a paw, pick up her paw for her and give it a shake. Then say, "Good shake!" and

Dogs need time to sniff each other. You don't want to pull them apart, because it can create social friction that can lead to fights.

This clever mixed breed has learned to give a high-five when he meets new people. It's more polite than sniffing their bottoms.

give her something to eat. Keep practicing, and have other people do it too. As long as there's the potential for food, dogs will remember this trick and try it every chance they get.

BREED SPECIFIC

All dogs rely on smells to understand the world and the people they're meeting, but they don't all put their noses in people's crotches. Large dogs are much more likely to do it, for the simple reason that their noses are at the perfect height to reach peoples' privates. Smaller breeds sniff what they can reach. The lowest smell center on the human body is the feet, and that's invariably what they go for.

Take her everywhere. Dogs spend most of their time at home, and when they do get out they're so excited and hungry for information that they can hardly keep their noses to themselves. Take them out in public more often so they meet a lot of new people. Eventually, they'll start getting blasé about the whole thing, in part because they'll have collected so much information in the past that they won't feel the burning need to collect more, says Bebiak. This will make it easier for them to remember to sit and shake rather than lunge and sniff.

FAST FIX Dogs despise the smell of minty breath spray, and you can take advantage of this to discourage them from sniffing people. When you're going to be in a situation in which your dog will be meeting new people, arm yourself beforehand with a canister of breath spray. When she moves in for the inevitable sniff, quickly spritz some of the spray toward her mouth. Aim downward so that the irritating spray doesn't hit her eyes. The unpleasant smell and taste, combined with the *psst* sound, is a very strong discouragement, Kovary says.

This type of "aversion therapy" works because dogs link the unpleasant experience with the behavior that caused it, and the memory will stay with them. For the most part, however, dogs learn fastest when they're praised for doing things right, rather than scolded for doing them wrong, Kovary adds. So reward your dog well when she sits and shakes. You should even reward her when she does nothing at all. As long as she's not sniffing, she's being a good dog and deserves a special treat.

CHAPTER TWENTY-TWO

HUMPING LEGS

It's All about Power

No one would mind if their dogs only humped other dogs at the appropriate mating times. It's how they reproduce, and if their level of discretion leaves something to be desired, well, dogs will be dogs. But some dogs aren't very selective about the objects of their affections. They'll try to hump arms, legs, teddy bears, sometimes even cats.

This type of indiscriminate humping isn't about mating. Even a dog who is frenzied by hormones knows the difference between a receptive partner and someone's leg. It's not even about pleasure, although that may play a role. Dogs mainly hump because they're trying to assert themselves. The longer they get away with it, the more powerful they feel, says Bernadine Cruz, D.V.M., a veterinarian in Laguna Hills, California.

Coming of Age

Humping usually starts during a dog's adolescence—between 6 months old and 2 years old, depending on the breed. This is the time when reproductive hormones

Dogs are always trying to prove that they're tougher than the next guy. Some do it by humping. Others do it by putting their feet on another dog's back, as this 6-week-old bulldog puppy is doing.

are starting to reach adult levels, and some dogs go a little bit crazy. "They reach sexual maturity before they reach emotional maturity," says Dr. Cruz. "They just don't know what to do with themselves."

Humping is not strictly a male behavior, Dr. Cruz adds, although males are the worst offenders. Unlike females, whose hormones ebb and flow with their reproductive cycles, males maintain fairly steady hormone levels all the time. The hormones themselves don't cause humping, but they make dogs more likely to do it. That's why neutering or spaying is the best way to reduce or eliminate this unpleasant behavior.

Young Rebellion

There's another reason that males are more likely than females to latch on to human legs, one that has nothing to do with reproductive urges. Males are just more competitive. They're always trying to prove—to people as well as to other dogs—how big and tough and independent they are. Humping is just one way in which they push the boundaries and assert their dominance within a family, says Dr. Cruz.

Watch a litter of puppies at play, and you'll see that they spend quite a bit of time climbing on top of each other. The more assertive dogs may take advantage of their position and throw in a little humping. It's their way of saying that they are, quite literally, top dogs. "They hump to show their dominance more than for any other reason," says Dr. Cruz. "My Pomeranian humps my Lab because she's much more concerned with rank than he is."

Once dogs are out of the litter and living with people, the same instinct remains. Human legs don't have special appeal, but they're accessible and easy to wrap paws around. "In the wild, dogs never mount dogs who are higher in rank than they are," Dr. Cruz explains. The only time that a dog tries this with people is when there's some confusion in his mind about who's in charge and who isn't.

It's not that dogs make conscious decisions to assert their authority. They hump as naturally as they bark or steal food off the table—it's just something they do. Even those who understand that they're not supposed to do it may forget themselves—when visitors come to the house, for example, or when people are on the floor

CALL FOR HELP

Dogs who hump people's legs almost always develop the habit when they're young. A dog who has never humped before but is suddenly doing it a lot should get a checkup because he could have a urinary tract infection. Humping may help ease the discomfort, says Bernadine Cruz. D.V.M., a veterinarian in Laguna Hills, California.

Humping is almost always a behavioral problem, Dr. Cruz adds. Dogs who hump legs and get away with it may experiment with other, more aggressive types of behavior. You should get some help, either from your veterinarian or from a professional behaviorist or trainer, if your dog doesn't give it up on his own.

playing with them. "If your dog wants to lord it over his stuffed toys or other dogs, you may not care," says Dr. Cruz. "But it's never okay for him to do it to a person."

Now That You Understand...

Give a motherly warning. You don't want to leave any doubt in your dog's mind that humping legs is a nasty habit. Discipline dogs the same way that their mothers would—by grabbing the scruffs of their necks, giving a quick shake, and shoving them away, Dr. Cruz recommends. "Don't try to lift your dog by his neck; but pull up that scruff, shake him quickly, and tell him no," she says.

Brandy Oliver, a dog-behavior consultant in Seffner, Florida, gives an even more specific command: She tells her dog, "No hump." "Now that I've had to use that command in some awkward situations, I wish that I'd come up with something else, like 'Play nice,' or 'Don't mess around,'" she adds.

Don't let him lean. Humping is generally the last link in a chain of physical liberties. Maybe your dog is always pushing against or leaning on your legs. Or he may insist on licking your face or climbing onto your lap. Physical pushiness is a sign that dogs are feeling free to do pretty much whatever they want. Once they get away with some aggressive physical contact, it's natural for them to push the boundaries further. You may want to encourage your dog to keep his distance, by pushing him away with your knee when he leans, for example, or by walking away when he's getting in your face, says Dr. Cruz. Once he understands that you only get physical when it's your idea, he'll be less likely to take liberties in other ways.

Let some air out of his ego. Dogs need to understand that no matter how exalted they feel around other dogs, they're always second banana in their dealings with people. Rather than dealing with the humping directly, it may be more effective to deal with the underlying attitude. Make dogs work

Dogs who are physically pushy—always climbing into people's laps or leaning against them—may take it one step further and start humping.

for everything they like, Dr. Cruz advises. Have your dog sit before you give him food. Have him lie down before you give him a toy. Have him do something—anything—before you do anything for him. When you reinforce your position of authority, your dog will be less inclined to be disrespectful.

FAST FIX It's rare for dogs to just walk up to someone and start humping. It usually happens when there's been a lot of excitement or physical contact—because someone is wrestling with them, for example. Keep games less physical while you're training your dog to keep his hips to himself, Dr. Cruz recommends. Physical contact is fine, but rough-and-tumble games may make it hard for him to remember what's he's not supposed to do.

CHAPTER TWENTY-THREE

DRINKING FROM THE TOILET

Cool, Fresh, and Tasty

Wine connoisseurs don't drink a fine Bordeaux from plastic cups. Draft lovers know that beer tastes lousy from cans. So it shouldn't come as much of a shock that some dogs like water best when it's served in a nice porcelain dish.

"To people, a dog who drinks from the toilet is just gross," says Ilana Reisner, D.V.M., Ph.D., a diplomate of the American College of Veterinary Behaviorists and a visiting fellow at Cornell University School of Veterinary Medicine in Ithaca, New York. "But to a dog, the toilet is a constantly freshened source of good water."

Before dogs had people laying out their food and water every day, they had to provide their own refreshments, Dr. Reisner explains. They developed a knack for choosing the cleanest, freshest water from the sources they had available. Those who didn't were sure to get parasites or other water-borne diseases. With no veterinarians or medications in sight, these dogs passed away. Those who learned the ropes, on the other hand, lived to reproduce, and their puppies instinctively knew what they should and shouldn't drink.

While their judgment certainly isn't perfect, dogs have good reasons for choosing the toilet bowl over their water dishes. Consider how people like their water: cool, freshly poured, and out of a clean glass. The toilet is probably in the coolest room in the house. The water in the toilet gets changed more often than the water in their bowls. And porcelain make a nice goblet that doesn't alter the taste of water like metal or plastic bowls may.

The toilet is just the right height for this American bulldog, who comes into the bathroom several times a day to get a drink. The water is cooler than in her bowl, and she seems to like the taste.

Feels like Home

People tend to be squeamish about bathrooms. We worry about germs. We scour and scrub to eliminate every last scent. We shut and lock the doors and demand total privacy. We do everything we can, in short, to keep our bathrooms separate from the rest of our lives.

Dogs, on the other hand, aren't squeamish at all. Consider their usual habits. These are animals who will eagerly sniff, roll on, and devour month-old roadkill. Who view cat boxes as convenient sources of takeout. Who greet each other (and people) by sniffing backsides. From their point of view, the bathroom is just an extension of their naturally earthy tastes. They don't think about off-putting odors when they drink from the toilet, says Reisner. If anything, they probably like the smell.

Cleaner Than You Think

There's no question that toilets are germy environments. Even an immaculate, freshly scrubbed bowl contains thousands, if not millions, of bacteria. But dogs don't care. After all, they didn't evolve in the dining room at the Plaza Hotel. For most of their evolutionary history, they lived in pretty rough surroundings. As a result, their immune systems are remarkably sturdy. Toilets may not be clean by our standards, but for dogs they're almost as hygienic as Perrier.

"A dog who drinks from a stagnant puddle, a lake, or a pond is exposed to more potentially hazardous germs than one who drinks from a toilet," says Dr. Reisner, who says she's never

CALL FOR HELP

Whether dogs drink from their appointed bowls in the kitchen or make detours to the commode, they always need to drink a lot of water—up to 5 to 7 percent of their weight every day. A 100-pound dog, for example, should have at least 5 pints (a pint equals 1 pound) of water a day, says Lynn Cox, D.V.M., a veterinarian in Olive Branch, Mississippi.

Dogs don't always drink as much as they should, however. Or, more commonly, they drink more than they should. Dogs who are suddenly drinking more than usual could have diabetes, kidney disease, or other physical problems, says Dr. Cox. This is why many veterinarians recommend keeping the toilet lid closed—not because the water is harmful, but because it makes it hard to tell when a dog's need for fluids has spiked upward.

Regardless of where your dog gets his refreshment, you should call your veterinarian if he's spending extra time at the water bowl, especially in cool weather or when he hasn't been particularly active, Dr. Cox advises.

heard of a dog getting sick from sipping potty water. This doesn't mean that dogs can't get sick from drinking toilet water, Dr. Reisner adds. A toilet that's stopped up or hasn't been cleaned since the Eisenhower administration will contain enough germs to trigger a day or two of diarrhea or vomiting. More worrisome than germs are chemicals. In our perpetual battle to keep bathrooms clean, we pour all sorts of chemicals into toilet bowls and tanks. Some of these products taste perfectly fine to dogs, but can make them ill if they drink enough.

Now That You Understand...

Even though toilets are sanitary enough for quenching canine thirst, most people prefer to keep the lids closed. Mainly, it's about etiquette. No one wants to listen to their dog noisily lap-

Some dogs become quite adept at opening closed toilet lids. The only way to stop them may be to weigh down the lid with something heavy, such as a large book.

ping up a toilet-water cocktail. And no one wants to clean up the trail of spittle and water that invariably follows.

Invest in a new water bowl. Some dogs drink out of the toilet because they like the taste. Others do it because they dislike the water in their regular dishes. It's not the water itself that's usually the problem, but what the water is served in. Plastic dishes, for example, absorb odors and may give water an off taste, says Dr. Reisner. Switching to a metal or ceramic dish—and washing it regularly—can make your dog's usual water supply a little more palatable—and make him less interested in finding alternatives, she says.

Put the bowl somewhere else. Dogs definitely like their water cool. Water that sits in a sunny kitchen may be 10°F warmer than water that's kept in a cool, tiled bathroom. If you don't have a different place to keep the bowl, put in a few ice cubes every time you change the water, says Lynn Cox, D.V.M., a veterinarian in Olive Branch, Mississippi. Dogs will appreciate the extra coolness as well as the crunchy ice.

FAST FIX The men in the family will undoubtedly need reminders, but the easiest way to keep dogs out of the toilet is to lower the lid. Unless, that is, you happen to live with a very smart and determined dog who learns to uncap the toilet on his own. If that happens—and some dogs like toilet water so much that wedging their noses under the lid is hardly an insurmountable obstacle—you'll either have to keep the bathroom door closed or secure the toilet lid by putting something heavy on top.

73

CHAPTER TWENTY-FOUR

DESTROYING FURNITURE
It's a Teenage Thing

It's remarkable what people will put up with. Carol Lea Benjamin, a dog trainer in New York City, remembers an overzealous husky who dug all the way through a couch. When his owners bought another couch, he tore that one up, too. Rather than buying couch number three, they called Benjamin, author of *Dog Training in 10 Minutes*.

"That was probably the most destructive dog I've ever seen," she says. "Two couches is pretty impressive. I told them that I'd be a lot cheaper than replacing more furniture."

Luckily, few dogs who set their sights on furniture run up that kind of tab. Most don't even need professional counseling. But they do need to learn that furniture is made for people to use, not for dogs to shred. And that can take some work and patience.

Something to Do When There's Nothing to Do

Nearly every dog was originally bred to do some kind of work. Working dogs were busy all the time. Dogs today, however, spend most of their time lounging inside while their owners are at work. They don't get as much exercise as they used to, and they get bored.

"The biggest reason that they start chewing, scratching, and ruining things in the house is because they don't get enough exercise,"

Benjamin says. Furniture is always accessible; it comes in an appealing variety of tastes and textures; and it's covered with great smells. Dogs with energy to burn and time on their paws may find it hard to resist.

"Dogs chew a lot of things just because they are there," adds Brandy Oliver, a dog-behavior consultant in Seffner, Florida. "Maybe your dog is leaning against the table leg. She gives it a lick. It doesn't taste bad, so she decides to take a chomp. Before you know it, it's a pile of splinters."

When high-energy dogs like this young American bulldog don't have enough to do, they get bored—and bored dogs often become destructive.

Mainly a Phase

Adult dogs occasionally tear up furniture, but for the most part this is a problem with younger dogs. When they're teething, for example, they'll chew on just about everything. Puppies aren't big enough to do a lot of damage. Dogs who are in adolescence—anywhere from 6 months old to 2 years old, depending on the breed—are the ones who tear things up the most, Benjamin says.

Adolescent dogs are a lot like human teenagers. They're somewhat wild. They seethe with energy. They haven't had a lot of training, and their hormones are driving them nuts. "People look at their dogs and all their problems around this time and ask themselves, 'What have we gotten into?'" Benjamin says.

Dogs do outgrow this destructive stage, but they can do a lot of damage in the meantime. Trainers often recommend applying a dog repellent such as Grannick's Bitter Apple to areas that dogs are abusing. It may help, but dogs who are truly driven to chew and destroy may not even notice that it's there.

Now That You Understand...

Keep an eye out for crumbs. In the age of television and Monday-night football, the couch has become the modern dinner table. Food invariably spills, and the alluring scents are the closest things to engraved invitations that dogs get. Once they start licking, chewing and digging are sure to follow, Benjamin says. Keeping a napkin on your lap and cleaning up crumbs before the odors get into the furniture will help prevent problems later.

Puppies need to chew to relieve the pain of teething. Once they get their teeth into furniture, they'll often keep at it and give it a thorough working-over.

Give her a toy box. Dogs sometimes get confused about what is and isn't appropriate to chew. Oliver recommends filling a small box with dog toys—rawhides, squeaky toys, tennis balls, whatever your dog enjoys. Put it right next to the furniture that she's been working over. "Every time she heads for the furniture, tell her, 'No chew,' then tell her 'Look in the toy box,'" she says. Most dogs will quickly learn what the words mean, especially if you get them started by occasionally salting the box with a couple of dog biscuits.

Keep her active. Dogs need a lot more exercise than most of them usually get. "If you can give your dog 10 minutes of exercise before you leave the house each morning, she'll burn off some of the energy that can make her destructive during the day," Benjamin says. Just as important, exercise provides bonding time that dogs need to feel secure—and secure dogs are the ones who are least likely to be destructive. "It would be great if we could all take our dogs to the beach for 3 hours on the weekend, but what they need more is to know that they're remembered," she says.

FAST FIX There's something about wood that dogs find hard to resist, and a table leg can be a lot more toothsome than an old rubber ball. Oliver recommends giving dogs sticks to chew. They're somewhat like bones—tough enough to provide tooth resistance, but soft enough to show results—and that makes dogs happy.

"When our dogs were puppies, we had hunks of sticks all over the house, but they never chewed the furniture," Oliver says. "If I had to choose, I'd clean up bits of stick again—they're much easier to replace."

This mixed-breed dog happily chews on his ball for hours. Like most dogs, he's less likely to chew furniture when he has an acceptable alternative.

An Indoor Excavation

PUPPY DOG TALES

Chewing and digging are nice, but smelling is even better. Getting to good smells, however, may require chewing and digging. Skye, a 2-year-old Chinook, proved to be a capable excavator when she was put in a room that contained the family's prized heirloom sofa.

It didn't take Skye long to realize that the sofa was a veritable mine of intriguing scents. She was determined to get to the bottom of things—literally, as it turned out. "She worked her way through the top fabric, right where our cat used to sleep," says Patti Cancellier of Rockville, Maryland, Skye's owner. "She went through the foam, down through the original fabric, all the way down to the old horsehair stuffing."

Within an hour, Skye had dug a hole that was $1^1/_2$ feet in diameter. Patti was appalled not only because of the destruction but also because her husband was home at the time of the excavation and didn't notice what was going on. But despite her irritation, she couldn't blame Skye. The sofa contained almost 100 years of scent history, and the little dog just had to explore.

Patti took pictures of Skye posing in front of the couch, just as a reminder of how much trouble puppies can be. Now that Skye has outgrown her chewing phase, Patti says, she's going to take a chance and have the sofa re-covered again.

The problem with sticks, of course, is the splinters. These aren't a problem for most dogs, but some dogs will actually swallow them. Watch your dog for a while. If she's content to just gnaw, she'll probably be okay. If she actually swallows the bits, you'll have to find something else for her to chew. Even a small splinter can cut her tongue or gums. Splinters can also damage her digestive tract.

CHAPTER TWENTY-FIVE

AFRAID OF CLIMBING STAIRS
Memories of Crash Landings

Nicki, a miniature dachshund, was sitting on the deck one afternoon when a black cat wandered through her yard. Her instinct was to chase, and in her excitement she forgot to be cautious on the steps. She paid for it by taking a painful tumble.

She wasn't seriously hurt, but mentally she was a changed dog, says her owner, Lois Ives of Norwich, New York. Nicki refused to set foot on stairs after that, and nothing Lois tried would convince her to ascend or descend on her own.

"Most dogs learn to handle stairs with reasonable grace and ease," says Benjamin Hart, D.V.M., Ph.D., professor of physiology and behavior at the University of California School of Veterinary Medicine at Davis and author of *The Perfect Puppy: How to Choose Your Dog by Its Behavior*. But some dogs never get the hang of it, or, like Nicki, they have a bad experience and never again feel comfortable climbing.

A Long Way Down

Dogs instinctively know that it's not a good idea to get too close to the edge of a cliff—and from their point of view, stairs can look an awful lot like a cliff when they're standing at the top, says Dr. Hart.

Most dogs encounter their first staircases when they're puppies. They're just as nervous as children encountering their first escalators. But after their initial apprehension, they're willing to take a chance. Gingerly at first, and with increasing confidence, they make their way up and down. It doesn't take them long to figure out that stairs aren't very hard to navigate.

Older dogs, on the other hand, can get very set in their ways. If they first discover stairs later in life, they're going to be reluctant to give them a try, no matter how much their owners cajole them. All they hear is the voice of Mother Nature, telling them they're standing on the brink and should forget about it. So they stay securely at the bottom or the top, refusing to venture onto that dangerous middle ground.

"It's harder for an adult dog who hasn't tackled steps before than it is for a puppy,"

CALL FOR HELP

Some dogs are truly afraid of climbing stairs, but others avoid them because they've developed arthritis or hip problems and climbing hurts, says Warren Liddell, D.V.M., a veterinarian in Norwich, New York. Arthritis mainly occurs in older dogs, and it can be treated with medications or, less often, with surgery. It's worth taking your dog in for a checkup if he has recently begun avoiding stairs, even if he otherwise seems healthy.

says Warren Liddell, D.V.M., a veterinarian in Norwich. The cut-off point seems to be about 6 months of age. Dogs younger than 6 months old are open to new things. Dogs older than that are conservative and not at all eager to take chances.

"Remember What Happened Last Time?"

Dogs learn from experience just as people do. And Nicki, a graduate of the school of hard knocks, took her lesson seriously.

"A dog who has fallen down a flight of stairs, even as a puppy, may remember it for the rest of her life and be nervous around stairs because of it," says Dr. Hart.

With the exception of dogs with physical problems such as arthritis, falling down a flight of stairs is unlikely to cause serious injuries. But that doesn't make them any more likely to re-member the experience fondly, says Dr. Liddell. Dogs who are unusually timid or nervous may be reluctant to ever put themselves in danger again. That's when owners find themselves in the position of having to choose between car-rying their dogs up and down stairs or giving in to the situation and allowing their dogs to stay on the ground floor all the time.

A Bid for Attention

Regardless of why dogs are frightened by stairs, the usual human response is to beg and plead with them to make the climb. This involves a lot of petting and reassurance. Dogs put two and two together very quickly. If making a stink

about ascending or descending brings the family running, any attention-loving dog is going to do it every chance she gets, says Judith Halliburton, a trainer and behaviorist in Albuquerque, New Mexico, and author of *Raising Rover*. This type of attention-driven behavior can be very hard to change. Dogs love the attention, but it invari-ably makes things worse.

"When we beg, plead, push, pull, or carry dogs up or down the stairs, they just get more apprehensive," says Halliburton. Even when the fears don't escalate, the theatrics do. Either way, the stairs become a psychological barrier that's difficult to overcome. At this point, you'll have to be more creative at getting them up and down on their own.

BREED SPECIFIC

Any dog can be afraid of stairs, but there's only one breed that's truly born to climb. The Norwegian lundehund was bred to hunt for birds called puffins that live in rocky cliffs. Over generations of breeding, lundehunds became increasingly adept at climbing. They even developed extra toes to give them better traction on the cliffs.

Lundehunds are rare today, in part because they were so successful. When puffins were declared an endangered species in the early 1900s, people stopped breeding lundehunds. Today, there are only about 2,000 lundehunds in the world. But they still have six or seven toes instead of the usual five, and they can outclimb any other breed.

Most dogs like food a lot more than they fear stairs. A trail of food ending with a delectable piece of hamburger will help most dogs overcome their nervousness.

Now That You Understand...

Put the best food out of reach. Dogs will do anything to satisfy their stomachs, which is why food bribes are very effective at getting them up and down stairs. The idea isn't to make the food easy to get, however. Put a so-so treat on the first or second step, a better treat a step or two higher, and something really great higher still, says Dr. Hart. Then stand back while your dog ponders what's really important to her. Sooner or later, her nose is going to lead her to the jackpot—and a dog who conquers stairs once will usually be willing to do it again.

Start with a single step. Sometimes fear is stronger than appetite. Dogs who won't climb stairs even to get a bite of bacon need more help. "When dogs face the staircase, they may see something insurmountable," Halliburton says. "They need to be taught to look at just one step and eventually go from there."

1. Just get their paws on the first step. It doesn't matter how you do it—with food, gushing encouragement, or anything else. Once they've made it that far, praise them like crazy, then walk away and do something else for awhile, Halliburton says. One challenge is enough for the day.

2. Then go up one level. It may take time and patience, but nearly every dog will be willing to mount that first step. After that, the rest is easy. Once a day or so, encourage your dog to take the next step. Make a big deal of it when she does. Then, as before, walk away and leave her to stay on the step or climb down, as she prefers. From a dog's point of view, climbing 2 steps isn't all that different from climbing 10. Helping her focus on the small picture—a single step instead of the whole staircase—will encourage her to take the chance.

CHAPTER TWENTY-SIX

HOWLING AT SIRENS
A Vaguely Familiar Sound

New Guinea singing dogs are famous for their ability to harmonize. These rare, wild dogs live on the isolated island from which they take their name. Unlike most dogs, who have been deliberately bred to have features such as wide-set eyes and docile dispositions, the singing dogs have evolved without interference from human beings. And they've spent about 6,000 years perfecting their singing skills.

"One dog leads, and the rest join in with an intricate chorus that runs up and down the scale," says Janice Koler-Matznick, an animal behaviorist in Central Point, Oregon, who studies the singing dogs. "It's like hearing a lead singer with a doo-wop group behind him."

The rare New Guinea singing dogs have a call that carries for miles. It allows them to keep in touch across the valleys of their mountainous homeland.

Nobody has to teach singing dogs to howl. They're born knowing how to. In fact, Koler-Matznick has seen a dog who was raised away from the pack sing perfectly in tune the day he met his peers.

To some extent, nearly every dog shares this rare breed's love of music. All that dogs need is someone—or something—to get them started.

Modern Sounds, Ancient Instincts

Anyone who lives in a suburban neighborhood has discovered that the wail of sirens is invariably followed by the wail of dogs. For a long time, experts believed that dogs howled at sirens because the high-pitched noise hurt their ears. But then people noticed that the dogs didn't seem to be in pain. If anything, they seemed pretty happy when they howled. And the louder one dog howled, the harder others would try to keep up.

It seems likely that dogs don't object to sirens at all. Rather, these neighborhood canine choruses are more like sing-alongs. Dogs who howl at sirens are reaching back into their genetic pasts. "The sound frequencies that dogs hear in the sirens probably are similar to the group-chorus howls made by wolves, coyotes, and other wild dogs," says Melissa Shyan, Ph.D., a certified applied animal behaviorist and associate professor of psychology at Butler Univer-

That's *Amore*

Any dog can howl, but Regal the beagle can truly sing. The distinction isn't always obvious when Regal is just sort of humming along, but his talent emerges when he launches into his full-throated version of "That's *Amore*." He brings more to his song than just volume. He can sort of carry a tune, too—at least you can tell that he's trying.

Regal's owner, Rachelle Divitto of Cleveland, didn't recognize his talent right away. For a long time, in fact, she thought he was complaining about her taste in music. But it was obvious that Regal was happy, not pained, when he howled. So like any good mother, she encouraged him to express himself.

Regal didn't howl at just any music, she adds. Most tunes left him thoroughly indifferent. But his favorites gradually emerged, and "That's *Amore*" was right on top. Whenever it came on, Regal would sit back, arch his neck, and start howling. Rachelle was impressed enough by his talent that she entered him in a singing contest called Search for America's Best Singing Pet.

This is why, one day in 1997, Regal found himself at the South Street Seaport in New York City, singing "That's *Amore*" for a crowd that included New York mayor Rudolph Giuliani. Regal won the contest, along with a private session in a recording studio and a featured spot in an advertisement for the contest's sponsor.

Regal's victory never seemed to go to his head. As far as Rachelle can tell, he's still singing his heart out just for the joy of hearing his own voice. But now he has an award to prove his talent, and that's worth something.

sity in Indianapolis. "Dogs are distantly related to these wild canines, and the sound of the siren triggers a deep-down instinct to respond."

The whole business is somewhat puzzling. When you listen to a police siren and then listen to dogs howling, it's hard to imagine that dogs actually confuse the two sounds. Most probably don't. All it takes is one dog getting duped into howling. Once he gets started, his neighbors have something real to respond to. So they join in. "It's a social event," says Dr. Shyan.

It's easy to understand why people were convinced that dogs were suffering headaches every time a fire engine went by. To human ears, it sure sounded as though they were in terrible pain.

No Practical Purpose

Howling made sense thousands and thousands of years ago. A howl can be heard a lot farther away than a bark can. Dogs who lived in groups and engaged in coordinated hunts needed to communicate with each other even when they out of each other's sight. Howling was a way of sharing important information like where they were, whether it was time to start a hunt, and when strangers were entering their territory.

Howling makes almost no sense today, however. In fact, dogs probably aren't even sure why they do it, says Dr. Shyan. But on some level, howling must be important, because dogs keep doing it. Judging from the enthusiasm with which they sing out, apparently it makes them feel good and allows them to declare their kinship with their buddies in the neighborhood.

BREED SPECIFIC

Basset hounds and beagles are among the most prolific howlers because they've been bred to chase prey and bark them into trees until the human hunters arrive.

Now That You Understand...

Give them something else to listen to. Dogs clearly enjoying howling more than people enjoy listening to them, and they aren't going to give it up willingly. But if you interrupt their songs, they may forget what they were doing. Crank up music on the stereo, Dr. Shyan recommends. This will interfere with the siren sounds that your dog hears and will give him less to respond to.

FAST FIX Apart from masking the sounds of sirens, a sudden blast of loud music is distracting. Dogs will stop howling to think about this new sound. That's the time to shift their attention to something else. Roll a ball across the carpet or flip them something to eat. The urge to howl usually passes after a minute or two, so a quick distraction is pretty effective at restoring quiet, Koler-Matznick says.

Teach them voice control. No one enjoys midnight howl-athons, but a lot of folks get a kick out of their dogs' natural musical talents. Most dogs will learn to sing after getting a few lessons.

1. Go into another room—or, if you're practicing outside, go a few yards away—and give a long, wailing howl of your own. Make sure your dog can't see you, Dr. Shyan says. If he can, he won't see the need to communicate by howling—he'll just come running over.

2. Make yourself sound wolfish by starting with a long howl, followed by several short yips—dogs' way of saying, "C'mon and sing with me now." Then be quiet for a few seconds to give your dog time to respond. If he doesn't, try a few more howls.

It may take a little time for your dog to figure out what the heck you're doing. But if he's a natural howler, he'll catch on quickly and will start singing along. "I have to hold my ears once I get my dogs started," Dr. Shyan says. "But they love to howl with me."

Although howling serves little practical purpose these days, many dogs still love to throw their heads back and give voice to the wild dog within.

CHAPTER TWENTY-SEVEN

SAYING HELLO BY JUMPING UP
Closing the Vertical Gap

At 6 weeks, a Great Dane standing on her hind legs is about a foot tall. Six months later, she's closer to 6 feet. That's a lot of dog to have jumping on you when you come through the door. Even if you live with a cocker spaniel or a Pekingese, jumping up is a lousy greeting. It ruins stockings. It gets muddy paw prints on your pants. And it bothers the heck out of people who don't want to get that intimate with your dog.

Here's the paradoxical thing. Yes, some people really dislike it when dogs, their own or someone else's, jump on them. But dogs, on the other hand, do it all the time because they think they're being polite. This is one of those cases in which human and canine expectations diverge, leaving bad feelings on the human side and disappointment on the dogs'.

A Problem of Reach

The next time you take your dog to the park, watch how she greets and is greeted by other dogs. They start by sniffing each other's mouths, then move around to sniff the back ends. All of this is considered proper and polite behavior among dogs, and they assume it's the way they should greet people as well, says Kimberly Barry, Ph.D., a certified applied animal behaviorist in Austin, Texas.

Here's the hitch. Dogs don't have any trouble sniffing our bottoms—they'd do it all the time, given a chance. But the first part of the greeting, the mouth sniff, isn't possible because we're so much taller than they are. Except for very short people with very tall dogs, the only way this is going to happen is if dogs get up on their hind

Part of the canine greeting ritual is to sniff and lick faces. Because people are so much bigger than they are, dogs try to bridge the gap by jumping up.

83

This Norwich terrier will do almost anything to get close to his owner's face. Jumping up won't get him high enough, so he's using his paws to get more reach.

legs or, in the case of small dogs, fly off the ground. They don't actually get a good sniff while they're airborne, of course, but their instincts tell them that this is a reasonable way to solve the problem.

Some dogs are more reserved than others in their greetings. Chows, Akitas, and Rottweilers, for example, are more standoffish than other breeds and rarely jump up to say hi to strangers. Terriers and golden and Labrador retrievers, on the other hand, will jump on just about anyone. And nearly all dogs will lovingly assault their owners if they think they can get away with it, says Sarah Wilson, a trainer in Gardiner, New York, and coauthor of *Paws to Consider.*

People have something to do with this as well. Dogs first learn their manners when they're puppies. Puppies are drop-dead cute when they put their little paws in the air, and most people make quite a fuss over them. So they keep doing it as they get older. What's cute in a puppy isn't very cute in an 80-pound German shepherd.

Oh, Does This Bother You?

With their thick fur and hard heads, dogs are a little like linebackers suited up for a game. They can slam into each other all day without feeling much of anything, because physically they're not very sensitive, says Wilson. They engage in a lot of full-body contact. "Often, they'll plow into other dogs the same way they plow into people."

Various breeds differ quite a bit in the amount and types of physical contact that they indulge in, Wilson adds. Toy breeds tend to jump up on their little legs and then hang on until someone picks them up. Greyhounds are more aware of their own physical space and usually keep a little distance. Retrievers, on the other hand, love contact. "They will slam into people, lick their faces, and be totally unaware that they've knocked you over and broken your glasses," says Wilson.

Now That You Understand...

Turn greetings into meetings. Dogs do their run-and-jump routines because they're so eager for attention that they can hardly stand it. So give them some attention. Turn the usual homecoming into a quick training workout, Wilson recommends. For a few weeks, every time you walk in the door and your dog jumps up, snap on a leash and practice some obedience drills. That is not what your dog had in mind when she came running over. It takes the edge off her excitement. "I practice 'sits' and 'downs' with them until they're absolutely sick of me," Wilson says. "They start to think, 'Gee, I guess I really don't need this much attention,' and they start to back off on their own."

Turn your head to the side. Everyone has had the disheartening experience of rushing to meet someone only to be met in return with profound indifference. It's enough to make you think twice about showing that much enthusiasm next time. Dogs react the same way, says Dr. Barry, who recommends giving your dog no attention when you walk in the door. Ignore the jumping. Ignore the pleading eyes. Sit down and read a newspaper. Give her a chance to settle down. At that point, invite her over and lavish her with all the attention you want. This teaches a valuable lesson: "I get ignored when I'm hyper, and I get my ears stroked when I'm calm. Hmm."

Pull them sideways. Leashes aren't only for going for walks. You can use them to teach dogs all sorts of things, including the benefits of staying grounded. Once again, this trick involves a little training. Once or twice a day, put a leash on your dog. You can either hold the end or let the leash drag on the floor. Then wait until someone comes to the door at an arranged time. The minute your dog launches her usual jump, grab the leash and pull it sideways. "The idea isn't to haul your dog off to the side, but to give enough of a pull to make her stop and think about what she's doing," Wilson says.

Dogs who jump up need to be kept on a leash whenever people are coming over. A quick tug on the leash will pull them off-balance and let them know that they're doing the wrong thing.

The sideways pull is critical, she adds. Dogs don't like being pulled off-balance. Your dog won't stop jumping immediately, but if you do this every time she jumps, she'll start to investigate other, calmer ways of greeting people.

FAST FIX Nothing gets a dog's attention more effectively than food, and dogs who are eating aren't going to waste time jumping up, says Brian Kilcommons, a behaviorist and trainer in Gardiner, New York, and coauthor of *Paws to Consider*. "Hold a treat at your dog's eye level when you walk in," he suggests. "Toss it off to the side as you head past her, and she'll learn to look for the treat instead of jumping up."

CHAPTER TWENTY-EIGHT

SAYING HELLO BY PEEING

Pure Emotion, Total Respect

People greet each other by making eye contact, shaking hands, and asking about the weather. More formal greetings—at Buckingham Palace, for example—might involve a curtsy or bow. For the most part, anything between "Hey!" and "Ma'am" is considered polite.

Dogs have greetings for different situations too. An informal introduction begins with a face sniff, followed by a sweeping sniff down the length of the body, and concluding with a sniff around the rear. When they're greeting someone they really want to please or someone who really intimidates them, they give the ultimate courtesy: They pee.

It's hard to imagine urine as a form of flattery, but among dogs it symbolizes tremendous respect, says Kimberly Barry, Ph.D., a certified applied animal behaviorist in Austin, Texas.

Dogs view every individual as being a little more or a little less important than the rest. To keep questions of rank crystal clear, dogs use body language to show respect to superiors and power to subordinates. They have many ways of expressing respect. Avoiding eye contact is one. Crouching down is another. When the message still isn't getting across, peeing on the floor clears up any ambiguity. It can be loosely translated as "You're the boss."

Together at Last

Splashes of urine aren't only a status signal. Dogs will sometimes urinate accidentally when they're so excited that they can hardly hold still. This usually occurs in young dogs, although adults sometimes do it too, says Sandy Myers, a behavior consultant at Narnia Pet Behavior and Training in Plainfield, Illinois. Part of the reason is bladder control—younger dogs don't have much. It doesn't help that the most exciting time of day—when their owners walk in the door—coincides with the time when their bladders are fullest. "It's a tough combination," Myers says.

When dogs want to show respect and submission, they go belly-up. They may even pee a little to reinforce the message.

Submissive peeing mostly occurs in dogs who lack confidence. You can boost the self-esteem of small dogs by making them feel taller. For example, put them on a table and run through a few obedience commands while they're up there.

It's easy to tell the difference between excitement and submissive urination, Dr. Barry adds. "Dogs who crouch down very low or roll on their backs are peeing to show that they're submissive," she says. "Dogs who greet you by jumping and wiggling around are peeing because they're overexcited."

My Apologies

The same dogs who urinate when they're excited also tend to do it when they get into trouble, says Myers. And they do it for nearly the same reason. While some dogs are tough as nails, most aren't. When the people they love raise their voices, they'll do everything in their power to make the people happy again. They can't write notes or send flowers, so they pee. It's the equivalent of saying, "Sorry, sorry, sorry."

Dogs do this with other dogs too, and for good reason. The bigger, madder, more intimidating dog immediately recognizes the humility in the gesture. She'll usually walk away, satisfied that she has made her point.

Now That You Understand...

Make them feel taller. Every dog has a little bit of a Napoleon complex. No matter how big or small a dog is, she wishes she were bigger. Dogs who are insecure are especially conscious of height. These are the ones who are most likely to splash the floor in the foyer.

You can't make your dog any taller, but you can make her feel taller—and this can work wonders for her self-esteem. Teach your dog to climb up on a picnic table or some other elevated surface outside, Myers recommends. Let her get comfortable, then practice a few "sits" or "downs." Better yet, bring someone—a person or another dog—over to meet her. "It's amazing how much a little height can do for a dog's self-assurance," Myers says.

Get low and reach up. Dogs read our body language in ways we can hardly imagine. Take a welcoming rub on top of the head. For people, this is a natural show of love. For dogs, however, it's a sign of domination, especially when it's accompanied by direct eye contact. Dogs who are nervous about confrontations will get even more nervous, and nervous dogs are the ones who tend to pee when their owners come home. Dr. Barry recommends abandoning the head rub and replacing it with a rub under the chin. This is how dogs greet older or more dominant dogs, and they view it as a very gentle salutation.

Come home quietly. People are just as happy to see their dogs at the end of the day as their dogs are to see them. But this isn't the best time for energetic greetings, Dr. Barry says. Coming home quietly and not making a fuss will go a long way toward keeping things drier.

Go out as soon as you come in. Rather than having your homecomings in the hall, Myers recommends opening the door, then immediately stepping back outside, letting your dog follow. The extra physical space will make your arrival a little less overwhelming, and your dog will also have a chance to relieve herself before she gets worked up.

Help her learn self-control. Unless your dog is still a puppy, it's unlikely that she's going to learn to control her bladder any better. But she can learn to control her emotions generally. The less excited she gets, the less likely she'll be to make a mess, Myers says. By far the best way to teach dogs to control their exuberance is to teach them basic obedience. For one thing, dogs who have learned to listen for instructions are generally calmer than those dogs without any training, she explains. Just as important, when your dog does start getting worked up, you can just tell her "sit" or "lie down." This is the canine equivalent of chill-out time. "They need you to set the tone by giving them something to do when they get excited," Myers explains.

FAST FIX Probably the easiest way to help dogs overcome their damp greetings is to ignore them when you come home, says Dr. Barry. This may sound coldhearted, but your dog really doesn't need you to fuss over her at that particular moment. In fact, showing total nonchalance will help her understand that homecomings aren't such a big deal after all.

This Hungarian vizsla is learning basic obedience lessons to help her control her emotions, which will also help her control her bladder.

For this to be effective, however, you can't give even a halfhearted greeting. Sail right past your dog when you walk in, Dr. Barry recommends. Act as though you don't see her. Sit down and read the paper. Do some dishes. Do not give your dog any energy at all. This will give her time to get used to your presence. Her excitement will taper off, and that's when you can spend some time together.

This "I-don't-see-you" technique is particularly effective if you accompany it by tossing a treat on the floor away from you as you walk in, says Brian Kilcommons, a behaviorist and trainer in Gardiner, New York, and coauthor of *Paws to Consider.* The lack of reciprocal excitement on your part, and that the fact that something very interesting just hit the floor, will give your dog something else to think about. By the time she remembers you, the edge will be off her excitement, he explains.

CHAPTER TWENTY-NINE

RAIDING THE TRASH

It's Mighty Tasty

For dogs who have figured it out, trash cans are like the corner coffee shop, the neighborhood diner, and an all-you-can-eat buffet rolled into one. There's only one difference, which has nothing to do with the quality of the food: Trash cans are completely self-service. Dogs get hungry, they take what they like.

Of all the mystifying things that dogs do, this is the easiest to explain, although it's among the hardest for people to swallow. "Dogs will do just about anything for food, and the trash can does not have the same negative associations for them that it has for people," says Tony Buffington, D.V.M., Ph.D., professor of clinical nutrition at the Ohio State University College of Veterinary Medicine in Columbus.

Dogs have good memories. A dog who has scored one good meal from a trash can is going to keep coming back. Some dogs play trash cans almost like slot machines. It doesn't matter how often they lose. They keep coming

Putting the trash can away in a cupboard isn't enough to deter tenacious scroungers. This Australian shepherd knows how to nose open the door to get to the good stuff inside.

back, hoping against hope for another big win. Sooner or later, they get one. Trainers refer to this type of now-you-win, now-you-lose scenario as intermittent reinforcement. It's almost better than winning all the time, because scarcity makes the heart grow fonder. For dogs, there's no stronger kind of encouragement than occasional victories, says Sarah Wilson, a trainer in Gardiner, New York, and coauthor of *Paws to Consider*.

Smells like Supper

Dogs have a far better sense of smell than people do, so you'd think they'd be even more disgusted by trash smells than we are. But there's no accounting for taste. "The fact that dogs have a more acute sense of smell doesn't mean that the same smells that send us running do the same for them," says Dr. Buffington. Quite the opposite. The smellier things are, the more dogs seem to like them.

The list of canine comestibles includes rotten meat, moldy bread, spoiled sour cream, and all the other things that make trash, well, trash. As

Dogs today certainly don't need the calories, but the instinct to get extra is thousands of years old. A lid is no protection.

long as it's potentially edible, dogs are going to be attracted to it, says Dr. Buffington. "I can't think of any natural smell that dogs really dislike," he adds. "They like it all."

The reason that dogs like practically everything comes from their evolutionary history. For eons, they were hunters and scavengers. To survive, they ate just about every terrible thing that you can think of. If it didn't make them sick—and in many cases, even if it did—they figured that it was better to eat now and ask questions later.

Survival isn't a factor anymore, but they continue to scavenge, and trash makes good pickings. The things they find there, however, may not be edible at all. "I once treated a dog who ate a can of sardines, can and all," says Donn W. Griffith, D.V.M., a veterinarian in Dublin, Ohio. It's not uncommon for dogs to get blocked intestines from things they eat, he explains. They also get liver problems or, when they tackle unusually hard items, broken teeth. "There's a whole host of physical problems that may be caused by eating garbage."

Now That You Understand...

It's difficult to keep dogs out of the trash because the rewards they find there are powerfully motivating—so much so that dogs have learned to raise tightly closed lids and even open pantry doors when trying to get at them. Since they aren't going to give it up voluntarily, you may have to try more creative solutions to keep your trash stashed.

Make the trash less rewarding. Just as good tastes attract dogs to trash, bad tastes may

BREED SPECIFIC

The dogs who get into trash the most are the ones who are tall enough to reach it, like golden retrievers and Rottweilers. Smaller dogs, such as Chihuahuas (right), are equally tempted but don't have the same opportunities.

keep them away. Try booby-trapping the trash with stuff that will assault their taste buds, recommends Julia Jones, a service-dog instructor for Canine Companions for Independence in Santa Rosa, California. For this to work, however, you have to use bait that smells good enough for them to approach but tastes bad enough to keep them away once they've sampled it. Here are some suggestions.

• Cut a hot dog into pieces and coat the pieces with hot-pepper sauce.

• Put a few slices of bread on top of the trash and give them a liberal dousing with vinegar.

• Dust the top of the trash with baking powder. It contains a compound called alum that is harmless but tastes terrible to dogs. Sprinkle it on when you go to bed at night. If your dog drops by for a midnight snack, the taste will send him packing.

Rig an alarm. Dogs understand that they aren't supposed to root through the trash, which is why they generally go after it during the day when people are at work or at night after we've gone to bed. Since you can't watch your dog all the time, you may want to set up an alarm. There are several ways to do this. One is to hang a chain of bells from the side of the trash container. The sudden jangle will do more than startle your dog. If you're lucky, he will think that the trash had something to do with that awful noise, and he'll decide to stay away after that.

Another type of alarm is a mousetrap-like device called a Snappy Trainer. Available in pet supply stores, it's designed to give a loud snap when it's jiggled. If you put it on top of the trash, when your dog comes around it will go off like a gunshot and scare the heck out of him, says Judith Halliburton, a trainer and behaviorist in Albuquerque, New Mexico, and author of *Raising Rover*.

Turn the bin around. Kitchens aren't always designed in such a way that you can put trash containers out of reach. What you can do, if the bin has a hinged lid, is turn it around so that the side that opens faces the wall. You'll still be able to get at it, but it will be harder for your dog to get into position to nose the lid open.

Lock the lid. Department stores sell locks that are designed to prevent toddlers from opening trash cans. What works for children works equally well for dogs, says Jones.

Give him an extra meal. Dogs aren't necessarily starving when they raid the trash, but they're much more likely to go after free food when their bellies are a little empty. Dr. Griffith recommends feeding dogs two or more times a day. Since dogs tend to go after the trash at night, feeding them before you go to bed may be enough to keep them out of the trash.

CHAPTER THIRTY

RUNNING AROUND AFTER BATHS

Better Than a Blow-Dry

Tazzie is a 2-year-old red Border collie who loves the beach but hates getting wet. "She's very happy to stand in water up to her ankles," says Dawn Curie Thomas, D.V.M., Tazzie's owner and a veterinarian in Santa Barbara, California. "Any wetter than that is too wet for her."

When it's time for a bath, Tazzie pulls out all the stops to avoid the inevitable. "I pull out the towels, and she just disappears," says Dr. Thomas, who is also the author of *The 100 Most Common Questions That Pet Owners Ask the Vet.*

"You wouldn't think that the house had a dog at all." Once she's been found, Tazzie turns into 50 pounds of dead weight, hoping that her owner will give up and go away. When the bath is finally over, Tazzie runs around like a mad dog, desperately trying to get dirty again.

School's Out

Even dogs who enjoy baths will usually emerge from the water with a burst of super canine speed. They shake like crazy, then lunge for something dry—carpets or couches when they're inside or patches of dirt when they're out—to rub and squirm against. Sometimes, they're dirty again before all their fur is dry.

"When you bathe dogs, you have them totally controlled," says Bernadine Cruz, D.V.M., a veterinarian in Laguna Hills, California. "When they finally get out of the water, they're like kids who have been turned loose on the playground after being cooped up all day."

Dogs don't like being forced to do things. Once baths are over, they celebrate by shaking and running around.

Most dogs don't get bathed very often, so it's a big event in their lives. Love it or hate it, they emerge from the water totally stimulated. They just have to have a little running frenzy to release some of that energy, says Dr. Cruz.

What's That Awful Smell?

The whole concept of baths is lost on dogs. They're perfectly happy when their skin and fur are well-coated with their natural scents and oils, along with whatever they've been rolling in lately. "The last thing they want is frou-frou perfume on them and water in their ears," says Dr. Thomas.

Dogs who tear around madly after baths are probably trying to make themselves smell more like dogs again, which is why they often roll their wet, newly clean selves in the dirtiest stuff that they can find. "They may be trying to get rid of the 'stink' of the shampoo," says Dr. Cruz.

If your dog gets truly manic, you may find that it's easier to take him to a groomer for his baths. A basic wash and dry usually costs about $20 for small dogs and $40 for larger dogs. Groomers have deep tubs, professional-quality combs and brushes, and a lot of experience keeping dogs under control. Your dog will be cleaner than you've ever seen him. Of course, he's still going to roll in the first puddle that he finds when he gets home.

Now That You Understand...

Give a dry bath. One way to keep dogs clean without the house-drenching frenzy is to give them waterless baths. Pet supply stores sell

POOCH PUZZLER

Why do dogs shake when they're wet?

Humans are the only animals who reach for towels when they're wet. Birds and nonhuman mammals, dogs included, get rid of excess water by giving themselves a good shake. They have to do it because the sensation of water on their fur (or feathers) is akin to having a tickle in the throat. It's irritating. Giving a vigorous shake is like have a good cough. It makes them feel better right away, says Benjamin Hart, D.V.M., Ph.D., professor of physiology and behavior at the University of California School of Veterinary Medicine at Davis and author of *The Perfect Puppy: How to Choose Your Dog by Its Behavior.*

Dogs do the most shaking when fur high on their bodies gets wet, Dr. Hart adds. In fact, researchers have found that the shake itself begins high up on the body, then works down to the toes, with the tail shaking last. A dog with wet ankles won't do anything more than lick off the moisture, while a dog who's soaked up to his ears will shake it all off.

All that shaking isn't so good for your walls, but it's very good for dogs. It removes a lot of water quickly, and it helps prevent health problems such as ear infections and skin irritations. So even though their mothers aren't telling them, "Get out of those wet clothes before you get sick," dogs instinctively listen to Mother Nature and do the next best thing.

a mousselike product that you rub into the coat then brush out. It cleans and softens the fur without leaving an oily residue, and it doesn't

Dry shampoos will clean dogs' coats without giving them a chance to shake everywhere. The shampoos are massaged in, a sensation that dogs prefer to being bathed.

require any water. Since it's more like giving a massage than a bath, dogs aren't as inclined to run around and get dirty immediately afterward, says Dr. Thomas.

FAST FIX An easy way to keep dogs clean is to dust their coats with a mixture of cornstarch and baby powder, then brush it through their coats. The powder soaks up skin oils and helps eliminate the usual "doggy" smell. Your dog will still run around afterward, but without a water-filled coat, he'll pick up less grit and grime than he would after a conventional bath.

Get organized and move quickly. Since dogs don't get a lot of baths, they always get worked up when you try to lift them into the tub or soak them with a hose. You can eliminate

some of the postbath hijinks by making baths less exciting and more business-like, says Jan Stewart, a dog groomer in Granada Hills, California.

• Before chasing after your dog and dragging him to the tub, set out everything that you need for his bath—the shampoo, conditioner, brushes, and towels, Stewart says. This way, you won't have to go looking for last-minute supplies, and your dog won't have time to have second thoughts about getting scrubbed. Moving quickly is essential.

• Wear your dirtiest jeans and an old T-shirt, or put on a swimming suit. You're going to get wet, whether you like it or not. You may as well be prepared for it.

• As soon as the bath is over, snap a leash onto your dog's collar and get him outside. There's no way to stop dogs from shaking and running around, but you can take them to a location where the mess won't be a problem.

• Keep them in the bathroom after the bath is done. The postbath burst of energy only lasts a few minutes and simmers down quickly. As long as you have an easy-wipe bathroom without fancy carpets or expensive woodwork, it's easiest to wash your dog, give him a quick towel off, then leave the bathroom and shut the door. He'll still zip around, but the mess will be confined and he won't have a chance to get dirty before his coat is dry.

CHAPTER THIRTY-ONE

PREFER HUMAN BEDS TO DOG BEDS

Status, Comfort, and Room to Roll

If dogs had the opportunity to sleep-test beds, you can imagine what the winners would be. Over there are the dog beds: lumpy, bumpy, and tucked out of the way somewhere. Over here are the human beds: big, soft, high off the drafty floor, and occupied by people. From a dog's point of view, they're the best real estate in the house.

"People's beds are great places for dogs to be," says Brandy Oliver, a dog-behavior consultant in Seffner, Florida. "They smell great, and they're a place dogs can go when they want some company."

Nearer to You

Dogs aren't solitary animals the way cats are. They have spent most of their evolutionary history living with families of dogs. When night fell, they all curled up next to each other, says Benjamin Hart, D.V.M., Ph.D., professor of physiology and behavior at the University of California School of Veterinary Medicine at Davis and author of *The Perfect Puppy: How to Choose Your Dog by Its Behavior*. Sleeping close together kept them warm. It made them happy and secure. Now that they live with people, they want to continue this time-honored and comforting ritual, he explains.

More important than comfort is closeness. Dogs get lonely when they sleep by themselves in a laundry room or basement. "It's the company that makes the bed the place to be," says Dr. Hart. "Some people want their dogs on the bed and encourage them to jump up. The praise dogs get for coming aboard is probably all the motivation they need to do it every night."

Left to their own devices, in fact, quite a few dogs would choose to sleep near the bed,

Human beds have lots of attractions for dogs. They're big, soft, and high off the ground—but best of all, that's where the company is.

but not in it. That king-size mattress offers the ultimate in comfort, but there's a lot of activity up there. People roll around. They shove with their legs. They hog all the covers. "A lot of dogs start out on the bed at the beginning of the night and wind up on the floor," says Dr. Hart. They may come up for the closeness, but they'll climb back down for more serious sleeping.

Height Makes Might

There's another reason dogs gravitate to the bed, one that has nothing to do with comfort or closeness. Imagine a small executive who sits in a very large chair. That's how dogs perceive the bed. In their world, height is power. A shy, retiring dog, for example, will be very careful about raising his head so that it's higher than a more-assertive dog's. An assertive dog, on the other hand, will stretch his whole body upward in order to appear taller than he is. Sleeping on the bed automatically adds a few feet to a dog's stature, and that can be quite a perk, says Sarah Wilson, a trainer in Gardiner, New York, and coauthor of *Paws to Consider*.

There's nothing wrong with indulging a dog's quest for upward mobility. You have to be careful, however, that he doesn't take advantage of what he perceives as his privileged status. He may start lording it over other pets—growling when the cat dares to climb up, for example. Some dogs go even further. "Since I'm as tall as the people," their thinking seems to go, "I'm allowed to grumble when they push into my spot."

"For people, the bed is just a place to sleep, but for dogs, it's one of the ways they figure out what their social status is in the household," Wilson explains. A dog who feels that he has

---

SWEET DREAMS

Dogs have gotten pretty spoiled lately. Rather than sleeping on cold ground the way they used to, they curl up on beds that are as cozy—and nearly as pricey—as anything humans buy.

Water beds. Dogs with arthritis or other joint problems will appreciate a heated, puncture-proof water bed, which comes with a removable, washable cover.

Cedar-filled beds. Sweet-smelling cedar is a natural flea and tick repellent. But cedar beds can be lumpy, and most dogs prefer a mixture of cedar and a softer filling.

Sleeping-bag beds. For dogs who like getting under the covers, sleeping-bag beds are just the ticket. They look just like sleeping bags, only they have flexible rings at the openings to keep them open. They're sized just right for small dogs.

Folded-blanket bed. An old-fashioned bed is one of the least expensive—and also one of the best. Take an old blanket, fold it a few times, and put it where your dog likes to sleep. Since blankets are filled with human scents, they provide the ultimate in doggy comfort.

special rights is going to keep pushing the boundaries. Today's mild grumble may turn into tomorrow's nasty growl. Dogs who get uppity because of their comfortable sleeping arrangements need to be taken down a notch or two, quite literally, she says.

A dog who's accustomed to sleeping in the bed isn't going to give it up voluntarily, she adds. Even if you don't let him up before you go to sleep, he's going to try to sneak up once you're asleep. The easiest way to keep him out of your bed is to make his own bed a very comfortable place to be.

Now That You Understand...

Put his bed next to your bed. "Though dogs can adapt well to sleeping by themselves, they like to be in the same room with their families at night," says Dr. Hart. He recommends putting the dog's bed next to yours. He'll be able to smell you. He'll hear you breathing. And he'll know he's important enough to share the same general space, if not the bed itself.

Make his bed bigger. "You can't expect a German shepherd or a Rottweiler to be able to stretch out on a 3-foot round bed and be comfortable," Oliver says. Even though dogs sleep curled up most of the night, they need additional room to spread out when they feel like it. The bed should be as long as your dog is when he's stretched full length. For bigger dogs, you may need to put two pillow-type beds side by side.

Spend some time in his bed. Dogs climb into bed with people because it makes them feel important. You can make their beds feel just as

Dogs are less likely to hog people's beds when they feel that their own beds are special. A visit from his owner—as well as a pet and a few treats—is enough to convince this Labrador mix that his own bed is the place to be.

special by visiting them yourself. "Sit on the floor and pet your dog while he's in his bed," Oliver suggests. Occasionally stashing a biscuit in his bed is a good incentive, too, she adds.

FAST FIX It's not really the contact with your body that dogs crave at bedtime, but all of the other sensory stimulations that come with the territory, smells especially. Oliver recommends taking one of your old blankets and putting it on your dog's bed. It's loaded with your personal scents, and that will probably be enough to keep him happy.

CHAPTER THIRTY-TWO

UNRAVELING TOILET PAPER

Always Good for a Laugh

If ever there's a time when dogs look like mischievous toddlers, it's when they're sitting on the bathroom floor surrounded by ribbons of toilet paper. The expression on their faces says, "Oh, did I do that?" Once they see you laughing, they'll happily tear into it again.

"They may start pulling at the toilet paper because they're bored or curious, but once

This Rhodesian ridgeback puppy likes nothing better than to run up and down the stairs until they're festooned with toilet paper.

they get going, it's just plain fun," says Janine McInnis, D.V.M., a veterinary behavior specialist in Dallas.

Toilet paper is fun because it engages all of a dog's senses, says Emily Weiss, curator of behavior and research at Sedgwick County Zoo in Wichita, Kansas. "Toilet paper is soft and light, and it flips and flutters," she points out. "The roll makes a great noise when dogs turn it. And best of all, the pile just keeps getting bigger and bigger. For dogs who are really captivated by visual stimuli, the ever-growing white thing they're making is a huge reward for pulling on the roll."

The Paper Chase

Dogs can entertain themselves for quite a while with a roll of toilet paper, but what makes it really fun is the reactions of their owners. Nearly everyone laughs when they see their dogs' antics for the first time, and their dogs remember that. "Even if you respond with a shriek, that high-pitched shout sounds a lot like a puppy's yelp," says Weiss. "It translates to 'Let's go play!'"

Unraveling the roll is just part of the game. The other part is running through the house with the paper flapping. That's the part a lot of dogs really enjoy, says John C. Wright, Ph.D., a certified applied animal behaviorist; professor of psychology at Mercer University in Macon, Georgia; and author of *The Dog Who Would Be King.* Toilet paper rolls aren't very firmly anchored. Dogs get a lot of satisfaction from working them free from their holders and showing everyone in the family what they've done, he says.

Not everyone appreciates replacing a roll of paper, only to see it in shreds a few hours later. But you should consider yourself lucky when you have a puppy who limits himself to this shred-and-chase game—it means he's not destroying something else, Dr. McInnis says. "It's a whole lot easier to clean up toilet paper than to replace carpet or hang new curtains or bring in a new couch. Usually, closing the bathroom door does the trick."

Now That You Understand...

Toilet paper isn't expensive, and it doesn't make too much of a mess. Most people don't mind when their dogs shred a few rolls. Of course, no one enjoys reaching for the roll only to discover that the dog, once again, has taken it away—or left behind a soggy, tattered mess that's only good for the trash.

Make it clatter. Most dogs outgrow this unraveling phase, but some keep doing it because it's so much fun. Discipline may not

help, because it only takes a few seconds for dogs to turn a roll of toilet paper into streamers—meaning, it's hard to catch them in the act. One way to discourage them is to set a booby trap, says Weiss. Put an empty can or two on top of the roll. Put a few marbles inside the cans. When your dog gives the paper a pull, the cans will tumble, making a noisy clatter. After a few frights, most dogs will be convinced that grabbing the roll isn't as much fun as it used to be, she says.

FAST FIX People don't always realize that toilet paper unrolls two ways. When you hang it with the loose end on the outside, it's easy for dogs to unravel it by giving a pull. A quick solution is to reverse the roll so that it hangs with the loose end facing the wall. It will still spin when your dog paws it, but it won't unwind. This takes a lot of the fun out of the game, Dr. Wright explains.

Another solution is to switch from a horizontal holder to one that holds the paper upright. The loose end won't hang down, and most dogs won't bother giving it a spin.

PART FOUR

"I Like the Good Things in Life"

The Passion for Food and Fun

Having fun and stealing the limelight are what dogs live for. Their playfulness is what makes them so great to have around. When you understand what they enjoy the most, you'll discover ways to make each day even better.

LIKE HAVING THEIR EARS RUBBED

It's a Chemical High

Duncan is a stickler for routines, especially routines that feel good. A 10-year-old bearded collie in York, Maine, Duncan has a none-too-subtle way of getting what he wants. Every morning at the same time, he gets up from his favorite place on the floor and sits on Karen Norteman's feet, which is about the last thing she needs as she's getting ready for her long commute to her job with a Boston computer company. But she has learned that Duncan isn't about to get up from his foot-squishing position and let her put on her socks and shoes until he gets what he's after. Since Duncan weighs about 47 pounds, she can hardly ignore him.

"When Duncan gets his ears rubbed, he moans and groans and sings like a musical instrument," Norteman says. "He likes to have his back rubbed too, but that doesn't give him anywhere near the ecstasy he gets around the ears."

Nearly all dogs loving having their ears rubbed. You wouldn't think this would be such a common phenomenon. After all, there are hundreds of breeds, and all of their ears are different. Papillons' look like wings, German shepherds' are sharp peaks, and basset hounds have big, hanging floppies. But they all love a little ear work just the same.

"It's pretty much universal," says Allen Schoen, D.V.M., director of the Center for the Advance-

This Great Dane's expression shows that he's a sucker for an ear massage. The ears are filled with nerves, and dogs like having them touched.

ment of Veterinary Alternative Therapies in Sherman, Connecticut, and author of *Love, Miracles, and Animal Healing.* "Dogs crave affection and touch from their owners, so a rub on the ears meets a basic need for communication."

Pure Nerves

Ears are one of a handful of nerve centers on a dog's body that are extra-sensitive to touch. The only other places that are nearly as sensitive are their bellies and the nooks between their toes, says Christine Makowski, D.V.M., a veterinarian in Landenberg, Pennsylvania.

When you rub a dog's ears, the pleasure she feels is intense. And the good feelings don't stop on the surface. Their ears contain nerve branches that extend to the internal organs, says Dr. Schoen. When you rub them, your dog doesn't just feel good on the top of her head. The pleasure comes from inside her body too.

Because the ears are such a hotbed of nerves, they're the primary target of people who practice acupuncture and acupressure. Putting pressure on the ears sends nerve impulses right through the body. "There's essentially an entire map of the body on the ear," Dr. Makowski explains. In fact, many acupuncturists only work on ears, because they can treat the whole body that way.

Chemical Bliss

It's not uncommon for dogs to get so relaxed and blissful when they're getting their ears rubbed that they slip into happy sleep. It's not only because they're feeling comfortable.

CALL FOR HELP

Unlike humans, who have fairly straight ear canals, dogs' ear canals make a few sharp bends. This means they are at high risk for getting ear infections. Dogs who have always loved having their ears rubbed but are suddenly wincing and pulling away probably have an infection and need to be checked out.

Rubbing the ears sends nerve impulses to the hypothalamus and pituitary glands, says Dr. Schoen. These glands secrete endorphins, pain-killing, feel-good hormones that make dogs feel relaxed, even euphoric. When you rub your dog's ears, she's essentially getting high on her own hormones.

So is the person doing the petting. Researchers at the University of Pennsylvania in Philadelphia, the University of California, Los Angeles, and elsewhere have found that people get a lot of the same benefits that their dogs do. Rubbing dogs' ears triggers a flood of human endorphins. This in turn helps people relax and even lowers blood pressure.

Not for Everyone

Just as people don't want strangers coming up and rubbing their backs, dogs are particular about who rubs their ears. It's not a matter of snobbery. It's just that dogs have their own ways of relating to each other. One thing of which they're very much aware is height. Dogs with strong personalities will deliberately put their paws or heads on top of other dogs' heads. They couldn't care less about the ears. They're just showing that they're big enough and tough enough to do it—it's a power move. Should another dog attempt the same thing with them, it's a declaration of war.

Dogs don't expect people to act the same way dogs do, but they instinctively get uncomfortable when people they don't know loom over them or reach down to rub their ears. It's a show of familiarity that they don't like. Once they know you and like you, of course, all this changes. They know that you have the right to rub their ears, and so they sit back and enjoy it.

Dogs with more laid-back personalities, on the other hand, are accustomed to having other dogs do the head-over-head thing. In fact, they'll invite it by tucking their heads, crouching down, and rubbing the tops of their heads under a more dominant dog's chin. It's their way of showing respect. Even if they've never seen another dog, they understand that people play the same dominant role and that their ears are fair game. This is true of family members, of course, but also of people they've never met before. Power isn't an issue, so they'll take all the attention that they can get.

Most dogs fall somewhere in the middle and are neither dominant or submissive. They'll accept ear rubs from people with whom they feel comfortable, but they may be a little nervous about strangers with outstretched hands.

Now That You Understand...

It's pretty hard to rub dogs' ears in ways they dislike. To launch them straight to cloud nine, however, you need to hit as many of the nerves as you can.

Starting at the base of the ear, hold the flap between your thumb and forefinger, Dr. Makowski suggests. Very gently pull the ear straight out from your dog's head, letting your fingers slide as you go. If you do that about four times, moving your fingers each time so they slide over a different section of the ear, you'll hit just about every hot spot, and your dog will be very, very happy.

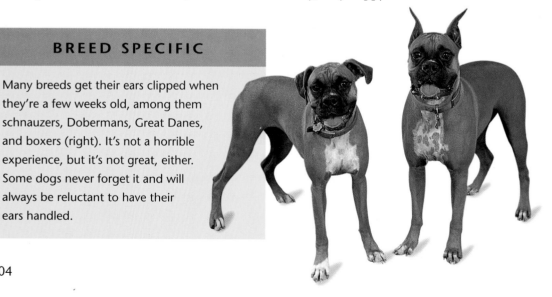

BREED SPECIFIC

Many breeds get their ears clipped when they're a few weeks old, among them schnauzers, Dobermans, Great Danes, and boxers (right). It's not a horrible experience, but it's not great, either. Some dogs never forget it and will always be reluctant to have their ears handled.

CHAPTER THIRTY-FOUR

LOVE HAVING THEIR BELLIES RUBBED

The Best Kind of Affection

When it's a belly rub she's after, Hazel knows exactly how to get it. In fact, the 7-year-old basset hound in Zebulon, North Carolina, has a routine that she follows night after night. She eats dinner. She asks for, and gets, three Meaty Bone treats. She takes a sip of water from her bowl. Then she hops her 48-pound self up on the couch, puts her head on a pillow, and rolls on her back—and scans the room for volunteers.

This terrier mix's idea of bliss is to sit on her owner's lap and to have her belly and chest stroked.

She doesn't have to wait long. Everyone in the family makes an *aw* sound and lines up to rub Hazel's lightly furred belly. Hazel, of course, eats it up.

Hazel isn't the only dog who does the belly-up routine. If there's such a thing as a universal pleasure center among dogs, it's the belly. The skin on their bellies is thinner than skin elsewhere, and there's not a lot of fur. As a result, the belly is exquisitely sensitive to touch, says Robin Downing, D.V.M., a veterinarian in Windsor, Colorado.

"One of the reasons we think of dogs as our best friends is that they have some remarkable similarities to us," adds Jeff Nichol, D.V.M., a veterinarian in Albuquerque, New Mexico. "They enjoy physical affection just like we do." A dog who's getting his belly rubbed enjoys the attention. He likes the nice sensations. And he likes knowing that he can attract people like a magnet just by rolling over and putting his feet in the air.

Ultimate Trust

Dogs use body language to convey very specific messages. Rolling on their backs and exposing their bellies is a sure sign of submission. It's a way of telling other dogs, "I'm at your mercy; do

105

Going belly-up is a sign of submission. It's how dogs express their trust and affection. It also feels good, as this Staffordshire bull terrier can attest.

what you will." A dog who's being threatened and wants to avoid a fight will expose his belly to signal his noncombatant status. Conversely, a dog who's at peace and relaxed will go belly up just because he feels safe to do so. "That position is the ultimate in vulnerability," says Dr. Downing.

People only reveal their softer sides to those they love and trust. It's the same with dogs. It takes a lot of trust for them to expose their bellies in front of people, and that's one of the reasons that belly rubs are such blissful experiences.

"When your dog looks at you, lies down, and flops over for a belly rub, that says something about the relationship you have with him," says Dr. Nichol. "It tells you that your dog knows that you are in charge, that he loves and trusts you, and that he's happy with that arrangement."

The unique thing about this behavior is that it presents one of the few opportunities that dogs have to set the agenda. "It's usually the people who decide when to spend time with their dogs," says Dr. Downing. "We choose when we'll go for a walk, when we'll take a ride in the car, when we'll sit on the deck and throw tennis balls. But here's an opportunity for dogs to say, 'I'd like to spend some time with you now.'" They know that their people will be more than happy to comply.

Selective Love

Some dogs are promiscuous with their affection. They'll roll over for anyone at just about any time. This is especially true of Labrador retrievers, who are known for their people-pleasing personalities. It's not uncommon, in fact, for Labradors to walk around a room, pause in front of each person they come to, and flop onto their backs.

Other dogs are much more cautious about revealing themselves. It's not a matter of love or affection, just one of temperament. "There are dogs who love you but who just don't want to be that vulnerable," says Dr. Downing. Her own dog, a 5-year-old pug mix, is a case in point. Despite his diminutive size, he's an assertive, dominant dog. He wouldn't dream of having his

Why do dogs kick their legs when you rub their bellies?

One minute, you're casually rubbing your dog's belly and he's lapping it up. Then, all of a sudden, your hand is caught in a windmill of whirling back legs and claws, driving you away. What makes a pleasurable belly rub turn into a leg kick?

Most of the time, it's because you've hit a tickle spot, says Jeff Nichol, D.V.M., a veterinarian in Albuquerque, New Mexico. The areas between and below the ribs are loaded with nerve endings, and when you hit several of these nerve endings at the same time, it tickles and makes dogs uncomfortable.

A reflex action may be involved as well. Just as your doctor can make your leg kick by rapping your kneecap, it's possible to make dogs kick by inadvertently hitting one of their many reflex points.

Dogs aren't uniformly ticklish. The same pressure and place that sends one dog's leg into overdrive may elicit nothing more than a happy sigh from another. You'll just have to rub different places and see what happens.

Now That You Understand...

Rubbing your dog's belly is about as foolproof as anything can be. "Once a dog rolls on his back, the message is pretty much, 'Touch me anywhere; I'm yours.' You can't do much wrong," says Dr. Nichol. Still, every dog likes having his belly rubbed in a slightly different way. Here are some of the pleasure points.

Rub where he can't scratch. Nearly all dogs love having their chests rubbed. This is partly because the chest and chin are areas that puppies lick when they want to show respect, and dogs instinctively respond to the gesture with affection. It's also a place that they can't scratch very easily. Rubbing the chest shows love and respect, and maybe relieves an itch or two at the same time.

Work on the bare belly. Because there's very little fur on the belly around the belly button, this is probably the most sensitive place to rub. Most dogs love it, says Dr. Downing.

Play with pressure. "Some dogs like to be rubbed vigorously, as though you were toweling them after a bath, and some prefer little strokes or circles," Dr. Downing says.

Most dogs are suckers for a belly rub, but dominant and reserved breeds such as Akitas (left) may not appreciate the intimacy.

belly rubbed. "As much as he loves me, he's just not that kind of dog," says Dr. Downing.

Akitas are known for being independent and somewhat reserved. They're less likely than most dogs to ask for or even tolerate a belly rub. The same is true of huskies, Alaskan malamutes, and other breeds with strong, assertive personalities.

CHAPTER THIRTY-FIVE

SITTING ON PEOPLE'S FEET

Better Than a Security Blanket

Dan Hickox's dog, Homer, is only truly happy when sleeping in one place—on Dan's feet. Homer stakes them out for midmorning daydreaming, afternoon naps, and nighttime snoozes. He doesn't care where the feet are. He sits on them when they're on the floor, on the couch, under the kitchen table, or on the bed—anywhere he can catch them staying still long enough for him to settle down.

There's no getting around the fact that dogs love feet and everything associated with them. They adore shoes and socks, and most of all, they love the smelly tootsies themselves. "Your feet are the part of you that your dog knows best," says Sarah Wilson, a trainer in Gardiner, New York, and coauthor of *Paws to Consider.* "They're right there on the floor with her; they're full of the smell of you; and lots of times, they're the only part of you that dogs are allowed to sit on."

One reason that dogs like feet so much is the same reason that most people steer clear of them. For such a small body part, feet pack a whole lot of scent. Each foot has about 125,000 sweat glands. That's enough to keep plenty of smells percolating, especially when the feet are encased in socks

and shoes. Dogs draw a huge portion of their knowledge of the world from their sense of smell. And feet sure do smell.

Close to You

Rich aromas aren't the only things about feet that dogs find attractive. They also depend on them as sort of a human tether. "There are some dogs who worry that their owners will get up and leave without them noticing," says Nicholas Dodman, professor of behavioral pharmacology

Large dogs, such as this chocolate Labrador, are too big to comfortably sit on laps the way small dogs can. Sitting on feet is the next best thing.

and director of the Animal Behavior Clinic at Tufts University School of Veterinary Medicine in North Grafton, Massachusetts, and author of *Dogs Behaving Badly*. "They don't want their people to get very far away, so they sit on them."

Large dogs are more likely than small breeds to choose a podiatric perch. Small dogs can scramble into laps when they want to keep track of their people. Big dogs are too bulky for that kind of cuddling. Sitting on feet gives them similar feelings of closeness and reassurance.

Of course, there are plenty of dogs who simply want to be near the people they like. They're not all that desperate for attention or reassurance—they just like the closeness. "You don't cuddle up with your husband on the couch because you don't want him to sneak away without you noticing," says Wilson. "You just like the physical contact."

Now That You Understand...

Some dogs crave foot contact more than others, and there's not much you can do about it. Keep your leather shoes in the closet and be grateful that your dog wants to be close to you. Dogs who are truly anxious about being abandoned, however, need some extra reassurance.

Schedule cuddle time. Dogs who know they can depend on getting attention at certain times of the day or in certain places are less likely to demand it the rest of the time. Set aside 5 to 10 minutes each day when your dog can sit on your feet, lick your face, and generally revel in physical contact, Wilson recommends. She'll come to depend on these regular meetings and look forward to them—and she'll be less

Feet are smelly and easily accessible—two factors that make them irresistibly attractive to dogs.

desperate the rest of the time because she'll know something good is coming.

Protect your space—but just a little. Dogs who are insecure are constantly crowding their people, and they can get frantic when the people are out of sight. The only way they'll feel more confident is if they're gradually weaned from clingy contact, says Rolan Tripp, D.V.M., a veterinarian in La Mirada, California, who specializes in animal behavior.

Once or twice a day for a few weeks, attach a leash to your dog's collar and tie it to something a few feet away from where you're sitting. You want her to be close enough that you're in sight, but too far away to make physical contact. She'll whine at first, but eventually she'll give up and lie down. As soon as she's been still for a minute, toss her a cookie and tell her how great she is. Most dogs catch on very quickly that a little separation can make the stomach fonder. Once they've figured that out, your feet will get a break, Dr. Tripp explains.

CHAPTER THIRTY-SIX

BITING WHEN PLAYING

So Excited They Can't Stand It

Boys ages 5 to 9 are bitten by dogs more than any other group of people—5 times more, to be exact. The reason that these poor kids seem to be bite magnets is that they're boisterous, aggressive, and seething with energy. In other words, they act a lot like young dogs, and young dogs bite each other when they play.

"Animals play much rougher than people do," says Betty Fisher, an animal behaviorist and trainer in San Diego and coauthor of *So Your Dog's Not Lassie*. This isn't a problem when they're playing among themselves. They have thick fur that protects them from each other's teeth. People, with their soft skin and hairless bodies, are much more vulnerable. Adult dogs understand this, but puppies don't. "When they get really caught up in a game, they can get carried away and forget who they're playing with," she says.

Dogs from 6 months to 2 years old do the most biting. Like human teens, they have more energy and strength than judgment. Plus, they're constantly testing boundaries, Fisher adds. Even when they know they're not supposed to bite, they'll try just to see what happens.

Dogs usually bite when everyone is running around and getting worked up, says John C. Wright, Ph.D., a certified applied animal behaviorist; professor of psychology at Mercer University in Macon, Georgia; and author of *The Dog Who Would Be King*. The faster and more furious the game, the more stimulated dogs get. At that point, they're prepared to match playful aggression with more aggression. And once they're caught up in the camaraderie and competition, they may forget all their good manners and do rude things, including jumping on people, knocking over lamps, and biting.

Their Mothers Didn't Raise Them Right

Some lessons need to be taught at home. For dogs, one of the most important lessons they'll

Even gentle dogs sometimes bite when they get overexcited, such as when they find someone to play with and chase.

ever learn is that biting is bad manners. Mom dogs and other puppies in the litter have a very effective way of discouraging bites. They bite back, giving a little extra oomph for emphasis. It doesn't take dogs long to learn that biting invariably invites stronger bites in return. By the time they're 8 weeks old, most pups have learned that biting their elders and playmates is a bad idea, even when they're playing. And most of them carry this knowledge into their human families.

However, if a puppy is taken away from his siblings and his mother too early—especially before 6 weeks of age—he won't have learned the proper etiquette about biting, says Dr. Wright. At this point, it's up to his human "littermates" to teach the lessons that the poor pup didn't get earlier.

It's not always easy to do, mainly because of instinct: Puppies have an instinct to bite, and people have an instinct to swat the of-

POOCH PUZZLER

Why do dogs lick after biting?

For proof that dogs have tender hearts, watch what happens when they accidentally bite someone: They'll quickly give the area a gentle lick. "When you cringe or act surprised, your dog will lick you to appease you," says John C. Wright, Ph.D., a certified applied animal behaviorist; professor of psychology at Mercer University in Macon, Georgia; and author of *The Dog Who Would Be King*. "It's not necessarily that he feels bad because he bit you, but because he sees you're upset."

fending muzzle. This teaches dogs two things, says Dr. Wright. "They find that they can stop someone from swatting them by biting their hands and holding them. Second, they may decide that any hands coming toward them are fair game for biting."

You Just Don't Understand Me

To their credit, most dogs give hints before they haul off and bite someone, says Dr. Wright. During play, they'll get progressively mouthier up until the point when they actually clamp down. More often, bites occur when dogs are sick of playing. They'll show their reticence by pointedly looking away from whoever is trying to engage them. Or they'll turn their backs or lie down and try to ignore what's going on. Anyone who ignores these hints is likely to get nailed.

Dogs also bite when they don't like the way someone is playing, Dr. Wright adds. For example, people have an inclination to pull dogs' ears or to roll them over and pin them down when they're wrestling. Some dogs will put up with this all day, but others won't stand for it. "Dogs are smart enough to figure out that biting is a quick and easy way to stop games that aren't fun," says Dr. Wright. "And once they find a strategy that works, they stick with it."

Now That You Understand...

Talk like Mom. Since dogs tend to bite when they're acting childish, you can often stop them by acting motherish, which means giving a low, authoritative *grrr*. Dogs hear this sound a lot when they're puppies, especially when

When dogs start biting too hard, one way to stop them is to blow on their noses. This young Rhodesian ridgeback doesn't like the sensation and is starting to back off.

they're nursing and their teeth start coming in. They take Mom's threats seriously, and memories of her warnings stay with them. Growls get their attention and make them think twice about what they're doing.

Turn your back. "If you want to show your dog that you don't like the way he plays, stop moving, extricate whatever part of you he has in his mouth, and turn your back on him," says Fisher. This sends a very clear signal that you aren't happy and won't play unless your dog learns to keep his teeth to himself.

Use an extension. Rather than letting dogs mouth your hands, it's better to use toys, towels, or ropes as intermediaries. Anything that puts distance between your hands and their mouths will work better than hand-to-hand—or hand-to-mouth—games, says Dr. Wright.

Play at your level. Dogs love it when people get down on all fours and wrestle, head butt, and generally roughhouse with them. Physical games are fun, but some dogs have a

natural tendency to be dominant. Seeing a person on all fours makes them think they're dealing with a doglike equal, one whom it's perfectly acceptable to bite, Fisher says.

Dogs have a natural respect for height, however. Keeping your head and shoulders higher than your dog's will help him understand that you're the one he needs to respect, not the one he's allowed to bite, she explains.

FAST FIX A quick way to extricate toys—or hands—from overeager jaws is to blow on dogs' noses. They find this quick blast of air very distracting and will relax their jaws. "If you and I were playing a game and I suddenly blew on your nose, you'd stop whatever you were doing and ask me what the heck I was doing," Fisher says. "It's the same with dogs."

BREED SPECIFIC

Border collies, shelties, and other herding dogs have a hard time controlling their mouths when they're playing. This is mainly because they've been bred to herd livestock, and biting is one of the tools they use.

CHAPTER THIRTY-SEVEN

CHASING BALLS

It Just Comes Naturally

Pet supply stores sell an enormous variety of toys—rubber tug-toys, pull ropes, and squeaky cubes, to name just a few. These high-end gizmos may catch people's eyes, but they often leave dogs yawning. As any child who has turned a stick into a spaceship can attest, the best toys are usually the simplest. And nothing is simpler than a ball.

"I have to watch my dog when we go to the pet supply store," says Carol Lea Benjamin, a dog trainer and author of *Dog Training in 10 Minutes*. "He'll pick up a ball and carry it right out of the store in his mouth."

Balls are so attractive, in fact, that larceny is common. Dogs in parks have been known to stake out the tennis courts, waiting for an errant ball to fly over. Little League games have been interrupted by dogs running into the outfield to grab slow grounders. And more than a few children have gone to bed crying because family dogs have shredded—or at least slobbered on—their favorite balls.

Born to Chase

Wild dogs—and their ancestors, the wolves—weren't stealthy, silent hunters the way cats are. They had to chase their suppers. The fastest, most-eager runners were the ones who got the most to eat, and they lived long enough to have plenty of puppies. Multiply this by a few thousand generations, and the result is an entire species with an instinct to run and chase.

Dogs certainly don't confuse a baseball in the yard with a running rabbit. But the love of chasing has been deeply bred into them. What

Dogs no longer need to hunt, but they still love to chase. Balls provide all sorts of fun—they can be chased as well as caught on the fly and rolled along the ground with the nose.

POOCH PUZZLER

Why do dogs prefer tennis balls?

Even dogs who are blasé about balls generally will get a happy gleam in their eyes when they're given a tennis ball. There's something about these colorful, fuzzy globes that dogs find strangely intoxicating.

This is partly because of the size. Tennis balls are small enough for most dogs to hold comfortably, and large enough so they don't slip down their throats, explains Carol Lea Benjamin, a dog trainer in New York City and author of *Dog Training in 10 Minutes*.

More important, tennis balls have a soft, spongy surface, which is perfect for picking up and retaining scents. "They get a very personal scent from the dog's mouth as well," she says. "They can smell that it's their ball."

Best of all, tennis balls have a springy texture that dogs adore. When they chew, the balls squish down, then pop right back. "That bit of compression is a great workout for their jaws," Benjamin adds. "Some dogs feel lost when they don't have a tennis ball to chew."

they once did for business, they now do for fun, explains Katherine Houpt, V.M.D., Ph.D., a diplomate of the American College of Veterinary Behaviorists and a professor in the College of Veterinary Medicine at Cornell University in Ithaca, New York.

Chasing is just one reason dogs love balls. Catching is the other. Many dogs have been bred to hold things in their mouths. A ball isn't as exciting as a downed duck, but the sensation of holding something is probably very satisfying.

Plus, dogs have the opportunity to carry balls back to their owners, and this makes them feel as though they're fulfilling their life's mission, says Dr. Houpt. It's precisely what their parents, grandparents, and great-grandparents did, and they're carrying on the tradition.

"One of the things that makes dogs great pets is that they're so adaptable," Benjamin adds. "They're born with a drive to chase prey. When they chase balls, they're translating that drive into a game instead."

Now That You Understand...

Play with bright balls. Dogs don't see colors very well, so it doesn't matter very much what colors the balls are that your dog plays with, as long as they're not green or red, colors which are hard for them to see. Also, they should be brightly colored rather than muted. Most of a dog's vision comes from structures in the eyes called rod receptors. Rods are only sensitive to black and white. Brightly colored balls stand out more against the background and are easier for dogs to see.

Throw balls across their line of sight. How many times have you tossed a ball right at your dog, only to watch him lose sight of it? There's a reason for this. Dogs' eyes are set farther apart than ours. They can easily see movement off to the sides, but they have a lot of trouble seeing things that are right in front of them. They'll have more fun with balls when you toss them across their line of sight rather than right at them.

Set aside some throwing time. Some dogs are born chewers and will work over a ball as

You can encourage reluctant dogs to come to you by using two tennis balls. Entice your dog with one ball, then throw it. Then use the second ball to encourage him to come to you again.

enthusiastically as they'll splinter a stick. Most dogs, however, won't even notice a ball that's just sitting there. If you want your dog to get the most fun out of his ball, you have to set aside some time for throwing it. "I play tennis with my dogs a couple times a week," says Inger Martens, a trainer and behaviorist in Los Angeles and author of *Paws for a Minute*. "I hit the balls, they chase them, bring them back, and line them up for me to hit them again."

Practice the two-ball technique. Since dogs often go bananas for balls, you can use them as motivators when you're doing basic training, Dr. Houpt says. Training with balls is actually better than training with food. Balls have no calories. They make it easy for dogs to get a lot of exercise. And they help dogs get used to watching your every move, which is essential when you're teaching obedience, she explains.

BREED SPECIFIC

Dogs who were bred for hunting and retrieving, like terriers and golden and Labrador retrievers, are the ones most likely to get excited about balls. Dogs bred for protection, such as Akitas, tend to be indifferent.

Balls are especially useful for teaching the "come" command, Benjamin says. This command is tricky because dogs who are playing and having a good time aren't always paying attention to the person at the other end of the yard. When you're holding a ball, however, you can be sure you'll have your dog's undivided attention, she explains.

She recommends using two balls. Hold one of the balls in your hand so that your dog can see it. When his eyes are riveted on you, tell him "come." Wait until he comes and sits in front of you. Then throw the ball. Maybe he'll bring it right back, and maybe he won't. It doesn't matter too much because you'll be holding a second ball. He'll want that one just as much as he did the first one. Tell him "come" again, have him sit, and then swap balls for another throw. Dogs love this game because they get a chance to run, retrieve, and play with you. After a while, they'll come running whenever they hear the word come, whether you're holding a ball or not.

CHAPTER THIRTY-EIGHT

CHASING THEIR TAILS
Might Be a Rabbit

Even though she has mellowed a lot since she was a puppy, there are two things that get Hopie, a 6-year-old dachshund, totally riled up. The first is when her owner, Cindy Poole of Roxbury, New York, gets the leash out in the morning. The second is when the school bus pulls up outside and crowds of yelling, giggling children pile out.

Hopie has to deal with her excitement somehow, and a few barks just aren't enough. So she chases her tail.

"Lots of dogs chase their tails when they've got energy and excitement that they don't know how to handle," says Alice Moon-Fanelli, Ph.D.,

clinical assistant professor in animal behavior at Tufts University School of Veterinary Medicine in North Grafton, Massachusetts. For some dogs, the big event is going outside after being cooped up all day. Getting out of the tub is always exciting. And the sight of a leash is a sure-fire call to action. "For some dogs, chasing their tails is something to do when they really don't know what to do," says Dr. Moon-Fanelli.

Why Turn to the Tail?

Dogs have all sorts of ways of showing excitement. They roll over and over on their backs. They jump up on their hind legs. They run around in circles and bark. These are all normal outlets for energy and excitement, and dogs do them all of the time. Tail chasing is less common. Researchers are not sure why dogs do it, but they suspect it may have something to do with their hunting pasts.

This bullterrier mix chases her tail from time to time just for the fun of it. For some dogs, however, tail chasing can become an emotional compulsion.

Dogs originally got their meals by hunting, usually small prey such as rabbits. Their brains and eyes are wired in such a way that they're intensely aware of quick movements. It's possible, says Dr. Moon-Fanelli, that some dogs catch a glimpse of their tails, get excited, and, without thinking about it, try to catch the pesky things. They rarely succeed, of course. So they keep trying.

"We don't have any reason to believe that dogs really think their tails are prey to be captured," says Dr. Moon-Fanelli. "But that basic instinct may be what gets them started."

All for Show

Even if dogs initially see their tails as bushy little squirrels, it shouldn't take them long to realize their mistake. Yet some dogs keep chasing—not just once or twice, but all the time. They may simply think it's fun, especially when the people they live with think it's fun too.

"Tail chasing is pretty cute when dogs first do it, and a lot of people make a big fuss over it," says Kathy Gaughan, D.V.M., assistant professor at Kansas State Veterinary Medicine Teaching Hospital in Manhattan. Dogs enjoy an appreciative audience. When they discover that something gets them a lot of attention, they'll keep doing it.

But this has a downside. Like actors who are always "on," some dogs get such a thrill from performing that they keep doing it even when the curtain is down. Tail chasing is hard work, and they run themselves ragged until they collapse in a panting heap on the floor. Then they get up and do it again.

CALL FOR HELP

Dogs who compulsively chase their tails have always been thought to have personality disorders. In some cases, however, the behavior may be triggered by seizures. Dogs who chase their tails even when they appear to be miserable or totally unaware of their surroundings may have a neurological problem and should be seen by a veterinarian.

Coping with Confusion

Dogs who chase their tails aren't necessarily as happy as they appear, Dr. Gaughan says. When they don't know how to deal with a situation, such as meeting a strange dog, chasing their tails acts as a distraction. It buys them time while they think about what they're going to do next.

This sounds like a silly way to cope with confusion, but people do similar things, says Dr. Gaughan. It's called displacement behavior. Suppose you're having an internal debate about whether to complain about the service in a restaurant or just to keep the peace and keep eating. While you're making up your mind, you may rap your fingers on the table or fiddle with the napkin. The physical activity is a stalling tactic, and it helps dispel some energy at the same time. Dogs who chase their tails may be doing something similar, Dr. Gaughan says.

Any stressful situation can lead to tail chasing, adds Char Bebiak, an animal behaviorist and head trainer at the Purina Pet Care Center in Gray Summit, Missouri. "Dogs aren't able to say, 'Hey, take a break; it's stressful,'" she says. "Instead, they turn to a behavior they know, as a way of calming themselves."

Dogs who chase their tails all the time may have a compulsive personality disorder, Dr. Moon-Fanelli adds. One clue is whether they do other odd things as well. For example, dogs who chase their tails also may chase shadows or the moving sunlight on the carpet. Or they'll groom themselves constantly. Compulsive behaviors can be quite serious, and often need medical treatment, she explains.

Chasing the Pain

Dogs do a lot of things that are utterly mystifying to people, but sometimes the underlying reason is the simplest one imaginable. Some dogs chase their tails because they hurt, and they want to give them a lick and bite for relief.

"Sometimes, a dog gets her tail caught in a door, stepped on, or injured in a fight, and no one even knows it's wounded until they call their vet because they're worried about the tail

> **BREED SPECIFIC**
>
> Probably because they're bred to have strong predatory drives, bullterriers and German shepherds are much more prone to tail chasing than other breeds.

chasing," says Dr. Gaughan. Once the problem is taken care of, the tail chasing will stop as well.

Now That You Understand...

It's good entertainment to watch dogs chase their tails, but you don't want to encourage it. There's no way to predict which dogs will do it for fun and which will become truly obsessed.

"It can be like turning something on and then not being able to turn it off," Dr. Moon-Fanelli says.

It's best for your dog if you totally ignore her when she starts chasing her tail. Don't tease dogs with laser light toys, either, Dr. Gaughan adds. These toys can lead to the same type of compulsive activity that tails can. In fact, some dogs have been known to go nearly crazy chasing sunbeams or even moving shadows.

Even dogs without tails find these appendages fascinating. If they can't chase their own, they'll go after someone else's.

CHAPTER THIRTY-NINE

CHEWING STICKS

It Keeps the Jaws in Shape

One look at a dog's mouth tells you that it was designed for serious business. Those intimidating teeth suggest this was a creature whose ancestors had to rip, tear, and crunch to get themselves fed. Holding those teeth are strong jaws, capable of biting with several times more strength than human jaws.

Shredding a stick isn't quite the same as tearing supper apart, but it's good practice: One reason dogs chew sticks is that it helps them keep their jaws strong, says Char Bebiak, an animal behaviorist and head trainer at the Purina Pet Care Center in Gray Summit, Missouri. At one time, they got nutrition from every part of their prey, including the tough skin and bones, Bebiak says. Dogs in the wild probably chewed on sticks just as much as modern dogs do, as a way of staying in shape for the next meal.

"Sticks let dogs really work their jaws. And even though they may not need to hunt anymore, the urge to keep their mouths strong hasn't diminished all that much," Bebiak says. That's why dogs today, whose food isn't much harder than a rice cracker, continue to chew sticks, sometimes covering the yard with piles of wood chips. It gives them chewing satisfaction that they might not get anywhere else.

Chewing sticks serves several purposes: It passes the time, helps clean teeth and give jaws a workout, and gives dogs the satisfaction of destroying something.

Even dogs who aren't thinking about chewing will often do it once they have sticks in their mouths, adds Jeff Nichol, D.V.M., a veterinarian in Albuquerque, New Mexico. Dogs put all kinds of things in their mouths—not just sticks, but stones, old shoes, and leaves. It's their way of exploring new things. "Once something is in their mouths, regardless of why they picked it up in the first place, lots of dogs just start chewing," he says.

Once they've chomped down, sticks provide instant gratification, he adds. They have a firm texture and a little bit of crunch, which dogs enjoy. Plus, they're relatively easy to shred, and dogs enjoy seeing that they're making progress.

Looks Right, Tastes Good

From the time they're puppies, most dogs are attracted to sticks more than most objects they come across. This is partly because wood is easy to chew, but it's also because of the shape—sticks look more or less like bones. Bones are what dogs would be eating if we didn't pour their food into ceramic dishes. They like the meaty flavors of bones, and the marrow inside is an excellent source of nutrients, Bebiak says.

Sticks don't taste at all like bones, of course, and dogs do know the difference. But sticks have their own appeal. They have a musky, earthy taste that seems to appeal to dogs. And of course, they can find them just about anywhere. "The logic seems to be, 'If I had a bone, I'd chew that. But since I don't, this will do,'" says Dr. Nichol.

Now That You Understand...

Veterinarians worry about stick chewing because dogs will occasionally swallow what they chew. A mouthful of splinters isn't likely to cause problems, but swallowing a large hunk of stick may. While some dogs do get overeager and gulp sticks as soon as they're small enough to swallow, most just chew and spit, so to speak, says Cynthia Jacobs, D.V.M., a veterinarian in Clarksville, Arkansas. Still, you'll want to be safe. Here are a few things to watch for.

Clear the yard of fruit branches. Dogs aren't very selective about the types of sticks they chew. This can be a problem if you have apple, pear, or other fruit trees. The wood has a rich, aromatic taste that dogs like, but it also contains small amounts of toxins that can upset dogs' stomachs, says Dr. Jacobs.

Other types of wood can also make dogs sick—in some cases, seriously so, says Dr. Jacobs. Branches from azaleas and trees such as black walnut, black cherry, red oak, black locust, yew, and red maple contain substantial amounts of poison. Dogs who chew enough of the wood can get very ill, she says. If you're not sure what type of wood your dog is chewing, keep it out of reach until you can make sure it's not one of the hazardous varieties.

Limit the size. If your dog is going to chew sticks, make sure they're too big to fit all the way in his mouth, Dr. Jacobs says. Smaller sticks have a way of getting stuck, and more than a few

Puppies need to chew to relieve the pain of teething. If they can't find sticks, they'll make do with a substitute such as a broom.

Small sticks may get swallowed or stuck inside dogs' mouths. The safest sticks to let them have are big ones, but remember to replace them before they're chewed into splinters.

dogs have found themselves with their jaws locked open because a stick got wedged inside. Big sticks have a way of turning into lots of little sticks, however. Once piles of debris begin accumulating, you'll want to clean them up before your dog has a chance to take them back into his mouth.

Make sure he's not a swallower. Most dogs just chomp and shred their sticks, leaving the wreckage on the ground around them. They don't actually ingest much, says Dr. Nichol. Some dogs, however, swallow what they chew. Besides the risk of choking or intestinal blockages, dogs who actually eat sticks sometimes use them in place of regular food. "Sticks don't begin to meet your dog's nutrition requirements," he says. "If he's making a habit of eating them, you should steer him toward a chew toy that he can play with but won't be likely to swallow."

BREED SPECIFIC

Rottweilers, Dobermans, and other "protection" dogs are among the most enthusiastic stick-chewers because they've been bred to work with their mouths. In addition, all of the retriever breeds are known for chewing.

FAST FIX If your dog is determined to chew and swallow sticks, you're going to have to keep him away from them and give him something safer. The problem with rubber toys is that a lot of dogs don't like them very much. A good alternative may be sterilized bones. Available in pet supply stores, sterilized bones are hard enough to last a long time, but they still have a little bit of give. And they don't break down into splinters or tiny bits, says Dr. Nichol.

The choicest sterilized bone, however, isn't going to taste anything like sticks—or bones, for that matter. That discourages a lot of dogs from giving them a try. You can overcome this by basting the bones. Soak them for 10 to 15 minutes in beef or chicken broth. The meaty flavor won't last long, but it will get your dog's interest. Once he starts chewing, there's a good chance that his instincts will kick in and keep him going. Once he's chewed the bone for a while, it will take on his personal scent, and that will make it even more attractive.

121

CHAPTER FORTY

EATING THE CAT'S FOOD

Stolen Food Is the Best, Especially When It Smells

For a couple of old fogies, Cocoa and Tar get along pretty well. Cocoa, a 10-year-old dachshund, and Tar, a 20-year-old black cat, peaceably share a house and a yard almost all the time. Conflicts only arise at mealtimes. Cocoa tries every trick in the book to score some of Tar's food. It doesn't matter whether there's food in her bowl or not; she always tries to get the cat's. She has tried being sneaky, bold, and begging, but neither Tar nor her owner, Renee Martin of Olive Branch, Mississippi, will let her get away with it.

Still, Renee can't help but be impressed with Cocoa's persistence. "If there's any way Cocoa can get that cat's food, she's going to try," she says. "She doesn't seem to care that she never wins. She keeps at it anyway."

Mmm, Sure Smells

At pet food companies, nutrition scientists and veterinarians put a lot of energy into making dog and cat food healthy. Taste is important, too, but more for cats than for dogs. Dogs have some pretty nondiscriminating ancestors, who were just as likely to eat something they found dead on the side of a ravine as something they hunted down themselves. They cared a lot more about filling their bellies than about how food tasted.

Cats are different. They're very particular about what they eat. In fact, some cats will literally stop eating if they can't have foods they like, says Joanne Howl, D.V.M., a veterinarian in West

Some dogs see cats as competitors for food and their owners' affection. Stealing their dinner makes dogs feel that they have the upper hand.

River, Maryland, and coauthor of *Your Cat's Life*. To create appealing meals, manufacturers use the best quality fish, meat, and other ingredients. More important, they make sure that cat food is really smelly, because cats won't eat it unless the odor announces itself loud and clear.

Dogs are attracted to cat food for the same reason they're attracted to week-old carrion. They like anything that smells. And cat food sure does smell. Given a choice between their nutritious but relatively bland food and that stinky bowl of cat food, they'll go for the cat food every time.

Even if cat food didn't taste and smell so great, dogs would probably go for it because they like variety, says Robin Kovary, director of the American Dog Trainers Network in New York City. "Dogs will put just about anything new, from cigarette butts to a Danish, in their mouths to check them out," she says. "Cat food is novel and it's yummy. That makes it pretty irresistible."

Friendly Competition

As if the tempting taste and aroma of cat food weren't enough of an attraction, dogs have another, more emotional reason for eating it. They're greedy for the good things in life—affection, attention, the best spot on the couch, and food. They view cats as rivals for all of these good things. If they can sink their teeth into their rivals' food, that's kind of like shopping with someone else's money.

"Dogs get jealous of cats," says Dr. Howl. "Eating the cats' food is a subtle way for a dog to get one over on them."

Actually, all stolen food tastes best, and a dog will happily raid another dog's bowl, even if the food is exactly the same as his own. "Dogs who want to show that they've got some authority in the house will eat the other dog's food first to make the point," Kovary says.

A Little Too Rich

Dog food is about 20 percent protein. Cats, who are carnivorous, need more protein—their foods are at least 30 percent protein. A dog who eats too much cat food is going to get diarrhea and an upset stomach. If he keeps eating it, he's going to get fat. His snacks from the cat bowl won't do his owners any good either, since cat food usually costs two or three times more than dog food.

The opposite scenario, that of a cat filching dog food, would be much more serious. Dog foods contain an amino acid called arginine, which cats can't digest. In fact, dog food can be life-threatening for cats. Since they very rarely eat it, however, this isn't likely to be an issue, says Dr. Howl.

Now That You Understand...

Dogs are predictable about committing the same indiscretions again and again. Once they develop a taste for cat food, they'll go to great lengths to keep getting it. Obviously, putting the cat's food in a bowl on the floor isn't going to stop them. Since cats are more agile than dogs and more adept at getting into places that dogs can't, it's easy enough to find places where the food will be safe from canine crooks.

Install a food protector. One way to keep the cat's food safe is to install a chain lock on a cabinet or utility room door. Depending on its length, such a lock will allow the door to open just enough to admit a cat, but not enough to let a dog get to the goodies inside. If you happen to have a very small dog, of course, this isn't going to work very well.

If your dog is truly committed to eating the cat's food, you may need to put the food behind a closed door—in a closet, for example—and install a cat door, Dr. Howl says. An easier solution may be to put a baby gate across the doorway to the kitchen or utility room. Install it so it's a few inches above the floor. The food will be protected and your cat won't have any trouble getting in and out. If you happen to have a dachshund or another short breed, put the gate close to the floor and attach a small ledge on top. This will let your cat hop up and over.

Put the food high. Cats are the Michael Jordans of the animal world. They can jump astonishing distances without running starts. Dogs, on the other hand, couldn't do a slam dunk if they tried. Putting the cat's food on a high shelf or bookcase won't inconvenience the cat at all—most cats, in fact, prefer eating up high—and your dog won't be able to get at it.

FAST FIX Cats are intrigued by small, enclosed places. You can take advantage of this to create a safe food stash. Turn a wooden box upside down—packing crates work well because they're sufficiently heavy that dogs can't easily tip them over—and cut out a cat-size hole. Your cat will be in and out of the box all day, playing as well as eating, and your dog won't be able to squeeze his muzzle through, says Dr. Howl.

One way to foil cat-food thieves is to put the cat's dish up on a high place. The cat will feel safer, and the dish will be harder for the dog to reach.

CHAPTER FORTY-ONE

PREFER RAWHIDES TO RUBBER TOYS

Chewing and Swallowing Beat Just Chewing

The difference between chewing on rubber and chewing on rawhide is like the difference between chewing bubblegum and eating candy. Gum is great, but candy—well, who wants gum?

This concept explains why expensive rubber toys tend to lie forgotten under cushions on the couch, while rawhide chews are eagerly grabbed the instant they hit the floor. Rawhide chews are made from cow or water buffalo skin. They taste salty and a little meaty, and they have a nice texture—just what dogs like. And because rawhides absorb flavors, manufacturers can add an extra something that rubber-toy makers can't: Tasty bastes such as chicken, beef, and peanut butter. Dogs eat them up.

Rubber, of course, comes from plants, and there aren't many dogs who will pick a plant-and-chemical-based product over one that's nice and meaty.

Food versus Fun

It's not really fair to compare rawhides to rubber toys. Even though they're both designed for chewing, rawhides are a type of food, and rubber toys are, well, toys. They're meant to be played with and chewed, not swallowed. It's not impossible for dogs to eat rubber, but most don't. What they will do is throw rubber toys in the air, chew them for awhile, then toss them around some more.

"Rubber chew toys have a lot of mouth appeal," says Joanne Howl, D.V.M., a veterinarian in West River, Maryland. "The companies that make them do some really clever things with the textures, shapes, and firmness to make them fun for dogs to carry around."

One thing that dogs like about rubber toys is the squeezy factor. The more they bite down,

A rawhide bone will keep this American bulldog occupied for hours. It also cleans her teeth and gives her jaws a good workout.

the more the rubber bounces back up. This gives jaws quite a workout, which dogs enjoy. But most dogs don't settle down to gnaw on rubber toys they way they do with rawhide. They play with them, and they want people to play with them. Rubber toys are great for throwing. They hold up better than tennis balls. They stay relatively clean in the backyard, and they're a perfectly acceptable pacifier for dogs who like having something in their mouths all the time.

People like rubber toys too. For one thing, they're nearly indestructible, although dogs who try hard enough can sometimes reduce them to little rubber bits in a few hours. It's cheaper to buy one or two rubber toys than bag after bag of rawhides. And unlike rawhides, which have calories, protein, and fat, rubber toys won't make dogs fat—no matter how much they indulge.

Now That You Understand...

Get the right size. "If you give your 120-pound dog an itty-bitty rawhide bone for a treat, he's going to swallow it in about 2 minutes," says Dr. Howl. Rawhide is safe as long as dogs chew it up before swallowing, but large pieces may get stuck in their intestines, she explains. This usually won't cause medical problems, but it can lead to diarrhea.

Rawhide packages usually specify what size dogs the treats are for. This is only a starting point, says Dr. Howl. Watch your dog to see how long it takes him to finish a chew. It should take 2 days or more. Anything that he finishes quicker than that is probably too small, and he's going to have tummy trouble.

Rubber toys are better than rawhides for outdoor use because they're resilient, less likely to harbor germs, and easy to wash.

Beware of bastes. Dogs love flavored rawhides, but some of the flavors may not love them back. Dogs who are sensitive to the ingredients in different bastes may get diarrhea or other digestive complaints, says Dr. Howl. Try giving your dog unflavored rawhides to see if things improve.

Restore the flavor. Some dogs will only chew basted rawhides. The flavors don't last forever, however. Once the baste is gone, dogs will often abandon the chews and ask for new ones. Rawhides are expensive, so it's worth restoring used chews to their former flavorful selves.

Mark Beckloff, co-owner of Three Dog Bakery treat shops, based in Kansas City, Missouri, has developed a number of bastes, such as low-sodium tomato sauce thinned with a little water and spiced up with cheese, or beef broth thickened with a little flour and water, or simply beaten eggs. Dip the rawhides in the baste, then bake them in a 250°F oven until the baste dries.

Dogs love all three flavors, which usually will have to be reapplied every few days.

Keep rawhide inside. Rawhides that have been chewed and slobbered on for a few days become magnets for bacteria. In fact, the diarrhea that dogs sometimes get after chewing rawhides is probably caused by germs that had a chance to multiply. Bacteria in the house are less likely to be a problem, so that's where your dog should do his chewing.

Rubber toys are perfect for outside chewing, adds Char Bebiak, an animal behaviorist and head trainer at the Purina Pet Care Center in Gray Summit, Missouri. Rubber is imperme-

able, so bacteria are unlikely to multiply. Plus, you can easily wash the toys whenever they get too grungy.

Make rubber better. For dogs who don't like or can't tolerate rawhide but still want to chew, you'll need to get rubber toys that have taste appeal. Toys such as Kong, available in pet supply stores, are designed to be stuffed with food, such as peanut butter or cheese. Rubber toys that smell and taste like a peanut butter sandwich are in a whole different league from plain rubber. Even when the food is gone, dogs will continue to gnaw, chew, and paw them to get to the flavors inside.

A DIFFERENCE IN TASTES

The reason that beef, chicken, and peanut butter rawhides are such big sellers is that people are convinced their dogs will like them. The dogs, however, wish that someone would ask their opinion for a change. It's not that dogs don't like beef and chicken. They do. But what they really, really like, and what their owners never seem to buy, is something a little more pungent: garlic.

The Pet Factory, a rawhide manufacturer based in Mundelein, Illinois, has tested untold numbers of taste combinations. The testers, of course, are dogs. The one chew that dogs love best is called the Field Chew, which has been basted with garlic, liver, and brewer's yeast. This is far from the company's top seller, however, because

people are convinced their dogs want something beefy. In addition, the ingredients, from a human point of view, are a little off-putting.

"We don't call it the 'Garlic, Liver, and Brewer's Yeast Bone' for a reason," says Doug Van Treeck, general manager of the Pet Factory. "No matter how great it tastes to dogs, it just doesn't appeal to people."

This may explain why one of the company's rawhide products has been flavored with vanilla. Vanilla is a ho-hum flavor for dogs, but people love the smell, so that's what they take home.

CHAPTER FORTY-TWO

PLAYING TUG-OF-WAR

The Thrill of Competition, the Joy of Chewing

Dogs start pulling almost from the time they're born. Their first instinct is to latch on to their mothers and pull—it gets the milk flowing. Then they pull on their littermates' tails. They pull on their blankets. They pull on everything they can get their mouths around, and they keep pulling throughout their lives. "You'd have a hard time finding a dog who'll walk away from a game of tug," says Kennon A. Lattal, Ph.D., a certified applied animal behaviorist in the department of psychology at West Virginia University in Morgantown. "The mouth is the only grasping tool they have available, and tugging is almost what they're designed for."

Winning the contest isn't just about getting possession of the Frisbee. It's a chance for one dog to prove his superiority over the other.

It's Good to Win

Dogs are just as competitive as people—maybe more. The games they love best nearly always have clear winners and losers. Losers come away from games knowing that they're a rung down on the social ladder. Winners come away with bragging rights.

Tugging is a wonderful game because there's no ambiguity at the end. One dog tugs and gains the prize. The other goes home empty-handed.

"If you have a dog who's very submissive, letting him win at tug-of-war can give him the confidence boost that he needs," says writer Steve Dale of Chicago, whose syndicated column "My Pet World" appears in papers nationwide.

Dogs who are unusually assertive, on the other hand, tend to win a lot at all games. They love tug-of-war because it's another opportunity to show how strong and talented they are. For this reason alone, it's a good idea not to let them beat you too often when you're playing tug-of-war, says Dr. Lattal. It will only feed their already overstuffed egos.

A Controversial Game

For every dog who loves tug-of-war, there's a trainer who's not so sure. Because it's such a competitive game, it can bring out a dog's worst instincts as he pits himself against his owner.

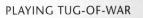

A dog who goes head-to-head with people may start thinking that their relationship is always a level playing field, and that's not an attitude that you want a dog to have.

Dogs with unusually dominant personalities or those who have shown signs of aggression probably shouldn't play tug-of-war at all, says Dr. Lattal. For most dogs, however, it's a healthy kind of competition. It gives them a chance to get physical and stretch their bodies. And it's an acceptable outlet for some of those canine urges that often get expressed in other, less acceptable ways.

"They can mouth all they want, slobber if they want, and pull as hard as they like, and it's all fine," says Dale. In fact, tug-of-war is about the only way that dogs can indulge two of their passions—chewing and interacting with people—at the same time.

Now That You Understand...

Choose your tug toy. Dogs who truly adore tug-of-war will start viewing everything as a potential toy. To avoid spending the rest of your life prying socks from your dog's jaws, pick one or two tug toys—a length of rope works well, as do the 2-handled rubber pullers sold in pet supply stores—and never use anything else, says Dr. Lattal.

Stack the odds. It's hard to play tug-of-war with strong dogs because, pound for pound, they're a lot stronger than we are. To keep the game from ending too quickly, use a tug rope that has a loop for gripping at your end and is tapered at the dog's end. This reduces the amount of pressure he can put into his grip,

Dogs love playing tug, but it's important to keep the game under control and to ensure that you win more often than they do.

giving you a distinct advantage. This may sound unfair, but your dog won't know the difference. More important, it ensures that you'll win most of the time, which will help your dog accept the fact that you're the leader after all.

Stop when you hear sound effects. Tug-of-war is always competitive, and it's normal for dogs to make little *grrr*'s when they're giving it their all. But growling has a way of turning into snarling, and snarling can lead to biting, says Dr. Lattal. Bites that occur during tug-of-war are usually accidental, but that hardly matters. They signal a level of aggression that's going to cause all kinds of problems—not just during the game itself, but in other ways.

Growling means it's time to stop the game, says Dr. Lattal. Put down the tug toy. Go into the kitchen to get a treat. Then make your dog sit before you hand it over. What you're telling him is that, regardless of the game, you're the one he has to listen to, and proper behavior and discipline are still expected.

CHAPTER FORTY-THREE

GETTING WET

It's Cool, Refreshing, and Filthy

There are dogs who like water and dogs who won't have anything to do with it. Then there's Dancer. A 3-year-old Landseer Newfoundland, Dancer loves water so much and swims so well that she could be a lifeguard. In fact, Newfoundlands are so adept in the water that breeders have developed a swimming test that human swimmers would struggle to complete. For Dancer to pass the test, she had to dive into a river and retrieve a life jacket and a cushion, in that order, that were floating 50 feet from shore. Then she had to swim 75 feet out to a rowboat with two occupants yelling for help, pass them a line, tow the boat to shore, and beach it. Finally, she had to "save" her own handler, Joyce Echon of Aliquippa, Pennsylvania, when she went into the water.

Labradors were bred to work in water. Like this puppy, they'll usually take every chance to swim or splash in whatever water they can find.

"Dancer has been swimming since she was 10 weeks old," Echon says. "She took to the water like a duck."

People have been breeding water dogs for a long time. These are the dogs who enjoy the water most. "Golden, Labrador, and Chesapeake Bay retrievers; Newfoundlands; and poodles all have strong histories with water," says Sandy Myers, a behavior consultant at Narnia Pet Behavior and Training in Plainfield, Illinois. "Their ancestors were bred because they showed enthusiasm for wading in without hesitation. After all, no hunter wants a retriever who doesn't want to get his feet wet in a swamp."

More Than Genetics

Much as people try to predict dogs' personalities according to their breeds, every dog is an individual. There are plenty of Labradors who hate getting wet and plenty of dry-dock dogs who will splash right in. "I've seen a West Highland terrier who'll dive into anything and swim underwater with his eyes wide open, and there are Labs who don't even want to take a bath," says Char Bebiak, an animal behaviorist and head trainer at the Purina Pet Care Center in Gray Summit, Missouri.

Since hunting isn't as popular as it used to be, many breeders don't worry if their dogs take to the water or not. The love of water has

become less of an innate characteristic than it used to be. Still, dogs keep getting wet. "They like water for a lot of the same reasons people do," says Vint Virga, D.V.M., a veterinarian at the College of Veterinary Medicine at Cornell University in Ithaca, New York. "It's cool and refreshing and fun to play with."

Deep in Muck

Even though dogs and people both like water, they differ in their choices of swimming holes. Give dogs a choice between a sparkling-clean swimming pool and a deep, murky, mucky puddle, and most will take the muck every time. No one is sure why they do it, but it's probably because way back in their evolutionary pasts, it made sense to cover their personal smells with something else.

"Just like hunters wear camouflage or special scents to conceal themselves from their prey, dogs may have an urge to put on the smells of their environment to make them blend in," Dr. Virga says. A dog who reeked of dirty water was essentially telling both prey and predators, "Ain't nothing here but a bunch of slime."

This may explain why dogs will fight like crazy when you give them baths, then rush to the nearest puddle as soon as you let them out.

Now That You Understand...

Dry those ears. Dogs who spend a lot of time in the water have a high risk of getting ear infections. Those with big, floppy ears, such as beagles and Labradors, have the highest risk because their ears trap moisture. Taking a minute

A big expanse of dirty water just adds to the fun of a game of chase for these three salukis.

to swab the insides of your dog's wet ears with the corner of a towel will reduce the risk of infections, Dr. Virga says.

Rinse their feet. Just as wet ears are prone to infections, wet feet can also be a problem, especially when dogs have been wading in dirty, bacteria-filled water, says Lynn Cox, D.V.M., a veterinarian in Olive Branch, Mississippi. He recommends rinsing your dog's feet with clean water after she has been wading. Or you can wipe the pads and between the toes with baby wipes.

Take your own water. Dogs who wallow in pond water usually drink a lot of it too. Their digestive tracts are much tougher than ours, and they're unlikely to get seriously ill. But even a mild infection can cause diarrhea, so it's worth giving them water from home. The more fresh water your dog drinks—adding $1/2$ cup of beef broth to a gallon of water will make it much more interesting—the less likely she'll be to imbibe a few quarts of pond water.

131

PART FIVE

"My Body Makes Me Do It"
When Anatomy Is Destiny

Living with dogs means encountering a wide-ranging spectrum of four-pawed faux pas. They don't mean to be rude. It's just that their bodies make them do things that humans wouldn't dream of doing.

CHAPTER FORTY-FOUR

AVOIDING HARDWOOD FLOORS
The Risk of Rollovers

It all started when Brendan Murphy of Olive Branch, Mississippi, dropped a grape. Francine, the family's yellow Labrador, scrambled to be the first one to get to it. She lost her footing on the hardwood floor and kicked it away instead. Determined, she lunged again. She slid straight into a wine rack, sending a red Bordeaux crashing to the floor. The startled, wine-spattered dog finally grabbed the grape, made her way through the rubble, and retreated to the relative safety of the carpet (white, unfortunately) in the next room to eat her prize.

Brendan, who's 6, thought it was pretty funny. "Francine didn't mean it," he said. "She just needs some practice on slippery floors."

Francine bounded right back onto the slippery wooden floor an hour later, but lots of dogs aren't so brave. After taking one hard fall, they may remain nervous about these treacherous surfaces for years afterward.

Clumsy by Nature

Anyone who's taken a turn on skates knows what it feels like for dogs to venture onto a hardwood floor. "It's how walking on ice is for people," says Benjamin Hart, D.V.M., Ph.D., professor of physiology and behavior at the University of California School of Veterinary Medicine at Davis and author of *The Perfect Puppy: How to Choose Your Dog by Its Behavior.* "Dogs have a hard time getting their footing, so they slip and slide. They know that if they fall, it's going to hurt."

Part of the problem is that dogs can't spread their front legs in order to get traction. When

Covering wooden floors with rugs or mats will help prevent dogs from slipping. The mats should have rubber backings for a better grip.

they try, especially when they do it quickly, it tends to hurt. After doing the splits a few times, they learn to avoid hardwood floors when they can. When they can't, they pick their way carefully across.

In addition, dogs don't have the kind of balance that people—or cats—take for granted. Their paw pads tend to be dry and callused, which reduces the amount of traction they can generate. And unlike cats, who have the ability to retract their claws, a dog's nails are always out, which reduces traction power even more, says Merry Crimi, D.V.M., a veterinarian in Milwaukie, Oregon.

Dogs who have grown up around hardwood floors know how to balance and have less of a problem, Dr. Hart adds. But those who are encountering them for the first time can have a hard time adjusting.

The Bigger They Are, The Harder They Fall

It's usually big dogs who have the most trouble with wood floors, says Jeff Nichol, D.V.M., a veterinarian in Albuquerque, New Mexico. Partly, this is because they have long legs and heavy bodies. When they fall, they fall hard. They also have a high center of gravity that works against them on slick surfaces.

"It's hard for them to stop falling once they lose their footing," Dr. Nichol says. "When a big, heavy dog lets one leg slip out from under him, it's going to go straight out, and there's not a lot he can do to stop it."

Another reason big dogs struggle with wood floors is that many of them have hip dysplasia,

CALL FOR HELP

Dogs who are most nervous about hardwood floors tend to be those who have other aches and pains and are wisely concerned about hurting themselves more. German shepherds, Labradors, and golden retrievers have a high risk of developing arthritis. Even if they don't fall, just slipping on a floor can cause a sudden jolt of pain, says Jeff Nichol, D.V.M., a veterinarian in Albuquerque, New Mexico.

If your dog is unusually gingerly about stepping on slick floors, or he's starting to have trouble getting up or getting around, he may have joint problems that need looking into. Veterinarians have begun doing hip-replacement and other types of joint surgery, but most dogs will improve with anti-inflammatory medications, Dr. Nichol explains. There are a number of new drugs that can reduce the pain and swelling of damaged joints without causing the side effects of some of the older drugs.

says Dr. Nichol. This is a hereditary condition in which one or both hip joints aren't as stable as they should be. Dogs with hip dysplasia may be a little clumsy, and the pain of slipping or falling is one they're likely to remember.

"Dogs who fall a few times are going to get anxious around the floors that trip them up," says Dr. Nichol. "They often get this head-down, hunkered-down, 'Oh, no, I've got to cross over this again' body language that tells you how much they hate it."

Now That You Understand...

Flip on a night-light. Dogs see a little better in the dark than people, but they're nothing like cats. Things that go bump in the night are often dogs trying to find the water bowl. The danger zones tend to be where carpets suddenly give way to wood floors. The unexpected transition from solid to slick can send them flying, says Dr. Crimi. She recommends using night-lights in areas where dogs have to walk across hardwood or polished linoleum floors. They're less likely to fall when they can see that the surface is changing, she explains.

Keep the nails short. Dogs with long toenails are at a disadvantage the minute they step on hardwood floors. The nails themselves are hard and skittery, and when they get long, dogs spread their toes slightly as they walk. This reduces stability and balance, says Dr. Nichol.

Most dogs need their nails trimmed every month or so. Older dogs need trims more often because they don't get as much exercise, which means the nails don't wear down as quickly as they grow.

Dogs dislike having their nails trimmed, so it's always a struggle to keep them short. You'll want to be conservative when doing the cutting. If you look carefully, you'll see a pink line, called the quick, extending from the base of the nail toward the tip. (For dogs with dark-colored nails, holding a flashlight to the nail will reveal the quick.) The quick is loaded with nerve endings and blood vessels. As long as you cut below the quick so that you don't cut into it, most dogs will learn to put up with occasional trims, says Dr. Nichol.

Make a path. Dogs who are perpetually slipping and sliding will be much happier if you make a path across hardwood floors, using rubber-backed mats or carpet runners. Don't depend on unbacked carpets or throw rugs because they slide around too much, advises Dr. Nichol.

Play on the carpets. It's fun to roll balls across hardwood floors and watch dogs go skating after them. Some dogs like this, too, but it's not a safe way to play, says Dr. Nichol. Slipping puts a lot of pressure on muscles, joints, and ligaments. And dogs who take a hard fall can damage their joints. Any game that requires running, twisting, or turning should be done on a carpeted area or outside, he advises.

A carpeted floor provides the best indoor playing surface for dogs. They can get traction and are less likely to slip and get hurt.

CHAPTER FORTY-FIVE

DOGGY BREATH

Bad Hygiene, Worse Appetites

Ebbie is a therapy dog who accompanies her owner, Cynthia Whittaker of East Meredith, New York, when she delivers Meals on Wheels to elderly neighbors. A 2-year-old yellow Lab, Ebbie has adoring eyes and a constantly wagging tail. Everyone looks forward to her visits.

Except for one thing: Ebbie's breath is rotten enough to curl hair, and her well-meaning kisses are often received with grimaces of disgust. Whittaker tried brushing Ebbie's teeth, but it didn't help at all.

Ebbie is hardly the only dog with horrific halitosis, which is why "doggy breath" has become a cliché for any odor that's unpleasantly pungent. Part of this is due to hygiene. We all know what our breath smells like when we

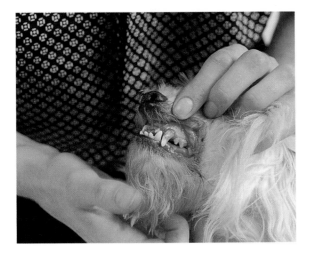

don't brush our teeth for a day, and dogs never brush theirs. In addition, dogs put their mouths in all sorts of places. They chew moldy tennis balls and lick their bottoms. They eat trash—and the older and smellier it is, the more they like it.

"If your dog helps himself to the cat box, then comes over and gives you a big wet kiss, you're going to smell it," says Robin Downing, D.V.M., a veterinarian in Windsor, Colorado. "That type of bad breath, mercifully, will go away on its own."

Bad Teeth, Bad Smells

For many dogs, however, the bad breath never goes away. Veterinarians estimate that nearly 90 percent of dogs have periodontal disease. This is a condition in which a bacteria-laden film called plaque hardens on the teeth, causing gum infections that often result in a rotten kind of smell, says Dr. Downing.

It's a fairly recent problem, she adds. Dogs who lived in the wild didn't live very long, usually 5 or 6 years. They weren't around long enough to get tooth decay. Dogs today live 12 or more years. The window of opportunity for

Gum disease, which sets in when food particles rot and harden on the teeth, is suspect number one when dogs develop persistent bad breath.

Small dogs like this Japanese Chin often have bad breath, because they have tiny jaws and close-set teeth that trap bits of food.

dental problems to set in—with the resulting smelly breath—is much bigger than it used to be.

Diets have also changed. Dogs get their food delivered in a dish. It's convenient, tasty, and easy to chew. So easy, in fact, that their teeth don't get much of a workout. As plaque accumulates, dogs' breath begins to stink. Contrast this to wild dogs. They were hunters. For their suppers, they tore apart chunks of meat and spent hours working over bones. Every meal provided tooth scrapings that a dental hygienist could only envy.

Finally, humans have bred dogs with small jaws and close-set teeth. Food particles easily get trapped, and infection in one place easily spreads to another. Tooth decay has become a real problem, and so has smelly breath.

I Can't Believe I Ate the Whole Thing

Dental problems are one cause of doggy breath, but they're not the only one. Dogs have table manners that, with all charity, can only be called gross. They stuff themselves silly, then release windy burps. They tip over trash cans and devour the contents. They eat discarded junk that they find on the sidewalk. It's not the healthiest diet, and their stomachs pay the price.

"You can tell how dogs are doing on the inside by how they smell on the outside," says Dr. Downing. "Bad breath that comes and goes is probably the result of temporary stomach upset or dietary indiscretions." Other internal problems can also cause bad breath. Dogs with kidney disease, for example, often have breath with a sour, metallic smell.

Now That You Understand...

Scour their teeth with rawhide. "Thick, knotted rawhide bones are terrific for dogs' teeth," says Dr. Downing. As the rawhide gets softer from being chewed, it works like a sponge to clean the teeth.

Dogs just adore trash and will pick it up from anywhere. Naturally, their breath isn't particularly sweet after a smelly snack from the gutter.

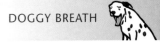

Encouraging dogs to drink after they've eaten will help wash away food particles that attract bacteria and cause bad breath.

What's good for the teeth isn't necessarily good for the stomach, Dr. Downing adds. Big dogs tend to swallow big chunks of rawhide, which can give them diarrhea when they eat too much of it.

Switch to a tooth-cleaning diet. A recently developed dry dog food called Hill's Prescription Diet t/d (the "t/d" stands for tartar diet) doesn't shatter like conventional kibble when dogs bite down. It stays partly intact. This means that each piece of food momentarily wraps around a tooth and scours the surface, Dr. Downing explains. It won't remove plaque that has already formed, but it will prevent new deposits from accumulating.

Buy clean-breath toys. Dogs who are chewers enjoy tearing into rope toys, which act like dental floss and clean between their teeth. In addition, pet supply stores sell chew toys with grooves and ridges. "If you put a little dog toothpaste in the grooves, your dog will brush his own teeth while he's chewing," says Dr. Downing.

Brush their teeth now and then. The best way to improve dogs' breath is to brush their teeth a few times a week. You can use a doggy toothbrush, but many people find that it's easier to rub the outer surfaces of the teeth with a small piece of gauze wrapped around a finger. (The inner surfaces are pretty much self-cleaning because they're constantly bathed with saliva.) Friction alone will remove much of the plaque, but you'll get better results using a toothpaste made for dogs. These come in appetizing (for dogs if not for people) flavors like malt and meat, Dr. Downing says.

Mix fresh vegetables into their food. It's too bad that dogs don't like parsley, because it contains compounds that act as natural breath fresheners. Fresh vegetables, however, are almost as good. Uncooked baby carrots and green beans clean the teeth—if your dog will eat them.

FAST FIX Dogs who drink water after eating are less likely to have bad breath, because water rinses away food particles that bacteria feed on. Dogs prefer fresh water, so changing it often is the best way to encourage them to drink, says Dr. Downing.

Veterinarians sometimes recommend flushing the teeth and gums with a Water Pik. An alternative is to let them drink directly from the hose, which many dogs enjoy doing.

CHAPTER FORTY-SIX

DROOLING WHEN THE FOOD BAG RATTLES

Too Excited to Swallow

Nearly 100 years ago, Ivan Pavlov and his dogs became famous worldwide for their demonstrations of what came to be called the conditioned response. Pavlov would ring a bell, then feed the dogs. After a while, the dogs started drooling the minute they heard the dinner bell, whether dinner was forthcoming or not.

Ever since then, everyone's assumed that food—or the mere idea of food—will make dogs salivate. It does, but so do many other things. In fact, dogs will drool almost anytime they get excited, says Jeff Nichol, D.V.M., a veterinarian in Albuquerque, New Mexico.

"If you've watched a 2-year-old at a Disney movie, you may have seen the same principle in action," says Dr. Nichol. "They get so wrapped up in the excitement of what they're watching, they just forget to swallow."

Research has shown that the salivary glands kick into overdrive when dogs (and people) start thinking about or actually smelling food. It's the body's way of starting the digestive process. But all sorts of thing can trigger a similar response. The anticipation of a walk or going for a ride will turn many dogs into veritable faucets.

"I had an Airedale once who stood in rapt fascination over a turtle for about 45 minutes," Dr. Nichol remembers. "And for 45 minutes, he drooled a steady stream on the floor. He just completely forgot everything else except what he was watching."

We often joke about people who can't walk and chew gum at the same time. That's actually a pretty good comparison of what happens with excited dogs. They can't concentrate and swallow at the same time.

Dogs often drool when they get excited. The sight of dinner being prepared is more than enough to start this mixed breed salivating. Other dogs may drool at the sight of sticks or the prospect of a walk.

Designed to Drool

Hot weather and simple physiology also explain why dogs get moist around the mouth. They respond to heat—as well as to stress—by panting. Their humid exhalations create a lot of moisture. Since they pant with their tongues out, all of that moisture runs downhill instead of backward toward the throat. Forget swallowing. They may lick their chops to mop up the moisture, but for the most part, they just drip, says Dr. Nichol.

Even dogs who don't drool very much in the kitchen may do it in the car. One of the first signs of car sickness—or anything else that upsets the stomach—is heavy drooling.

Drooling tends to be exaggerated in basset hounds, bulldogs, Saint Bernards, mastiffs, and

Some breeds, such as Newfoundlands, drool more than others because they have loose lips that catch saliva and frequently overflow.

Great Danes. These dogs have been bred to have pendulous lips. This has created little pockets inside the mouth that act as drool basins, explains John Simon, D.V.M., a veterinarian in Royal Oak, Michigan, and author of *What Your Dog Is Trying to Tell You*. It's not that they drool more than other breeds. It's just that the lip pockets frequently fill up and overflow.

Now That You Understand...

Withhold the leftovers. A dog who drools at the rattle of kibble is going to drool even more at the prospect of steak scraps or other fatty leftovers from the human table. It's not merely great-tasting food that causes heavier salivation—rich foods can upset a dog's stomach. A simpler diet won't stop drooling, but it may reduce the deluge somewhat.

Dress him in style. Tying a bandanna around your dog's neck is an easy way to blot the moisture and keep the fur on the chest dry. Fold the bandanna in half, corner to corner, and tie it around your dog's neck so that the triangle hangs over the chest. Bandannas look stylish and will go a long way toward keeping the fur—and your pants legs and the furniture—a little drier.

Provide a place setting. Since dogs do their heaviest drooling when they're eating (or waiting to eat), you may want to buy a package of paper place mats and put them under your dog's bowl. You'll have fewer puddles to clean up when he's done.

CHAPTER FORTY-SEVEN

LICKING THEIR FEET

Nearly Everything Makes Them Itchy

Imagine going through life without being able to scratch certain parts of your body. People are lucky in this regard. We have long arms and fingers that can reach just about anywhere. It isn't so easy for dogs. Despite their flexible spines and mobile hind legs, there are spots that they can't reach very well, such as the tops of their noses, the bases of their tails, and especially the bottoms of their feet.

Dogs' paw pads are loaded with nerve endings and are unusually sensitive, says Jeff Nichol, D.V.M., a veterinarian in Albuquerque, New Mexico. "When dogs get itchy, the feet are the place most likely to be affected." Since they can't use one paw to scratch the other, they use their tongues and teeth, and the biting and slurping can go on for hours.

There are several reasons that the feet are so prone to itching. For one thing, dogs don't wear shoes, which means their feet come into contact with all sorts of irritating, itchy things. In addition, they get allergies just as often as people do.

Dogs can be allergic to many things, and it's mostly their feet that feel the effects. Even walking or lying on newly mown grass can be enough to make them itchy, and they'll bite and lick their feet to get relief.

The main symptom of canine allergies is itchy feet. What they're allergic to doesn't matter all that much, Dr. Nichol adds. Food, pollen, dust, and fleas are all potential allergens that seem to affect the feet worst of all. Some dogs get itchy feet just from walking across a newly mown lawn.

Pause for Pedicures

Unlike cats, who happily spend hours grooming themselves each day, dogs are singularly grungy. They don't worry much about dirt. In fact, they seem to go out of their way to get dirty. Despite this general indifference to hygiene, they take very good care of their feet. At least a few times

a day, they inspect their feet closely, then lick and bite away things that happens to be stuck, like pebbles, burrs, or splinters, says Craig N. Carter, D.V.M., Ph.D., head of epidemiology at Texas Veterinary Medical Diagnostic Laboratories at Texas A & M University in College Station.

Normal foot grooming shouldn't take more than a few minutes, Dr. Carter adds. Dogs who lick or bite their feet all the time aren't simply being clean. There's something wrong, and they're trying to get relief.

Despite their passion for keeping their feet clean, dogs don't like it when anyone else touches them, says Dr. Carter. This may be because the feet are somewhat ticklish. It's not uncomfortable when they lick their own feet, but they don't want anyone else to do it. Even when they're among other dogs, the feet are off-limits. It may be that they have an instinctive aversion to having their feet handled.

"A dog's feet are everything to him," Dr. Carter adds. "Dogs depend on them to survive, so it's no wonder that they're protective about letting anyone touch them."

Now That You Understand...

Soak them in oatmeal water. The colloidal oatmeal sold in pharmacies is very helpful for reducing itching, says Dr. Nichol. Put a few inches of cool water in the tub or a basin, mix in a handful of the oatmeal, and let your dog stand in the solution for a few minutes. Even if you don't add oatmeal, cool water shrinks blood vessels in the feet, which will help reduce itching.

Protect the skin with fatty acids. Some dogs get itchy feet because they aren't getting

CALL FOR HELP

Allergies themselves are usually mild, but the way in which dogs react to them can be a real problem. Some dogs lick and bite their feet for hours, day after day. The constant moisture and friction can result in deep, hard-to-heal sores called lick granulomas. The sores are painful and often get infected, and they rarely respond to home treatments. Any sore on the paws that doesn't start getting better within a few days needs to be treated by a veterinarian.

enough fatty acids in their diets. Fatty acid supplements, available in pet supply stores and from veterinarians, can be very effective. They don't work quickly, however, so it may be a month or two before you notice any improvement.

Ask your vet about food allergies. People who are allergic to the proteins in certain foods will usually get hives or upset stomachs. Dogs with food allergies are more likely to get itchy feet. The only way to tell if your dog is allergic to something that he's eating is to put him on a totally different diet—one that contains none of the ingredients in his usual food. You can buy hypoallergenic foods from veterinarians and in pet supply stores. If food allergies are the problem, the itching should clear up in 8 to 10 weeks. At that point, ask your veterinarian to recommend a food that's less likely to cause itching later on.

Use antihistamines. Allergies can be difficult to identify, and some veterinarians don't

Petroleum jelly applied to dogs' paw pads once or twice a day will create a barrier against itch-inducing allergens.

Get rid of fleas. Flea bites themselves aren't very itchy, but some dogs have allergic reactions to flea saliva. The easiest way to get rid of fleas is usually with either an oral drug such as Program or a topical liquid called Advantage. Both of these products will control fleas much more effectively than sprays or powders, says Dottie LaFlamme, D.V.M., Ph.D., a veterinary nutritionist with the Purina company in St. Louis.

Don't bother with bad tastes. A traditional (and ineffective) remedy for foot licking is to coat the paw pads with a bad-tasting ointment such as Grannick's Bitter Apple. While this and other repellents may keep dogs away from your shoes or the furniture, they won't help with foot licking, because the itching is usually too intense—dogs aren't going to let a little bad taste get in the way.

bother. Instead, they advise treating the symptoms with antihistamines. Diphenhydramine (Benadryl) can be very helpful, says Dr. Nichol. He recommends giving 1 to 2 milligrams for every 8 pounds of weight.

FAST FIX Coating your dog's foot pads with petroleum jelly once or twice a day will help trap moisture and keep them from cracking and itching, says Dr. Carter. Unlike most hand creams and lotions, petroleum jelly also creates a strong physical barrier that will help keep molds and pollens off the pads.

BREED SPECIFIC

Despite their tough appearances, Dobermans and German shepherds (right) are real pussycats when it comes to sore feet. They're no more likely than other breeds to have foot problems, but they do tend to be more sensitive to pain and will complain more.

CHAPTER FORTY-EIGHT

SMELLY GAS

It Depends on the Menu

All mammals produce intestinal gas, and dogs are no exception. Compared to cows, which produce upward of 60 quarts of gas a day, dogs are relatively modest in their output. What they lack in quantity, however, they make up for in pungency—their gas is unusually smelly. Even a small dog can clear a large room, and bigger dogs, especially those who are real food-hounds, can be downright unpleasant to be around.

"Part of the reason we notice dogs' gas so much is that dogs haven't been taught to hold it in," says Dottie LaFlamme, D.V.M., Ph.D., a veterinary nutritionist with the Ralston Purina Company in St. Louis. "They don't go out of the room to pass it."

Protein In, Smells Out

The intestinal tract is filled with bacteria that help process foods and aid in digestion. As part of their natural metabolism, the bacteria release clouds of sulfurous gases, which gives intestinal gas its unpleasant smell. The more protein there is in the diet, the stronger the smell.

Cows and other herbivores produce a lot of gas, but there isn't enough meat-based protein in their diets to create large amounts of sulfur gases. Dogs, on the other hand, eat a lot of protein—quite a bit more than most people, says Dr. LaFlamme. They don't necessarily have a lot of gas, but when they do, it's powerful stuff.

It's not only protein that contributes to high-octane gas—it's also the type of protein. Many commercial dog foods get their protein from animal by-products—feathers, for example, or ground-up bone. These ingredients are harder for dogs to digest than protein that comes from "whole" foods, such as chicken meat or eggs, says Dawn Curie Thomas, D.V.M., a veterinarian in Santa Barbara, California,

Dogs love human foods, but their bodies often can't cope with them. The result is often more gas than usual—and it will be smellier than usual, too.

and author of *The 100 Most Common Questions That Pet Owners Ask the Vet*. The harder the body has to work to process protein, the more flatulent a dog is going to be, she explains.

Food Allergies and Sensitivities

A surprising number of dogs are sensitive to ingredients in their food. For example, milk is a common ingredient in dog food, but many dogs have a condition that makes it difficult for them to digest it. This condition, called lactose intolerance, can make dogs extremely gassy, says Dr. LaFlamme.

Food allergies are another problem. Dogs who are allergic to ingredients such as soy or wheat aren't able to digest their food efficiently and tend to be gassy. They often get diarrhea as well.

One way to tell if your dog is sensitive to something in his diet is to write down every single thing he's had to eat within the 24 hours preceding the gassy episodes. Sometimes something as simple as switching to a different brand of treats will make intestinal gas a little less unpleasant. Your veterinarian may recommend putting your dog on a diet called an elimination diet. He'll be given a hypoallergenic food containing ingredients he's never had before. If the gas goes away, you'll know that something in his food was causing it.

Now That You Understand...

Switch to a premium food. Sometimes just switching from a low-cost dog food to a premium brand such as Innova will reduce gas, says Susan Wynn, D.V.M., a veterinarian in

Switching to a premium food that contains high-quality ingredients will usually help decrease dogs' flatulence.

Marietta, Georgia. Read labels before you make the change. What you're looking for is a food that lists whole ingredients such as chicken, beef, lamb, and egg at the top of the ingredient list. If you see the word by-products among the first few ingredients, you'll know the food is going to be more difficult to digest.

Experiment with flavors. Every dog reacts differently to different foods. If you notice the gas is increasing when your dog eats a beef-and-potato-based food, switch to one with lamb or rice, or even one containing venison or rabbit and potato.

Ask your veterinarian about lower-protein foods. Since it's mainly protein that makes a dog's gas so smelly, you may want to switch to a lower-protein food, especially if your dog has been eating a high-performance chow. Some foods supply more protein than dogs need. You can cut back without compromising good nutrition. Protein is a key ingredient in

Fewer rawhides can mean less gas. Dogs who swallow bits of rawhides, rather than just chewing them, often get gas from the excess protein. In addition, the large amount of air that they swallow while chewing them can also cause flatulence.

every diet, however, so talk to your veterinarian before making the change, says Dr. Thomas.

If you do decide to change foods, do it gradually. Dogs who are suddenly switched from one food to another tend to get diarrhea, says Dr. Thomas. You can make the transition more comfortable—and less gassy—by adding a little bit of the new food to your dog's usual diet for a few days. Each day, gradually increase the amount of the new food while cutting back on the original. You'll know in a month if switching foods is going to help, she says.

Take human foods off the menu. Dogs will eat just about anything, but their bodies aren't designed to handle most of the foods people eat. "Table scraps are often the culprit," says Dr. LaFlamme. "If you're slipping your dog bologna or cheese or ice cream, that may be what's causing the problem."

Get rid of the rawhides. Dogs love these tough, chewy little treats, but rawhides don't always love them back. They're very high in protein, and dogs who eat a lot of them tend to get gassy—not just because of the protein, but because they swallow buckets of air while chewing them, says Dr. LaFlamme. Give your dog some other treats for a few weeks and see if the air improves, she suggests. Or give him larger, tightly tied rawhide bones, which take longer to eat.

Give digestion a hand. You can buy a gas-reducing product called CurTail in pet supply stores. It's a digestive enzyme that helps break down foods in the intestine, leaving less fodder for gas-producing bacteria, says Dr. Thomas.

Feed your dog more often. Dogs who eat their food all at once tend to have more gas than those who eat smaller amounts more often, says Dr. Thomas. She recommends feeding dogs two, three, or even four times a day. Your dog will still be eating his usual amount, but spreading out the serving times will help the intestines work more efficiently, she explains.

BREED SPECIFIC

Many German shepherds have a hereditary condition in which they don't produce enough digestive enzymes. This doesn't necessarily affect their overall nutrition, but it can result in foul-smelling gas. Other gassy breeds include boxers and bulldogs. These dogs have short, flat faces and short respiratory tracts. They gasp quite a bit and tend to swallow air when they eat, which can result in extra gas.

CHAPTER FORTY-NINE

LIFTING THEIR LEGS WHEN THEY PEE

Hitting Heights for Bragging Rights

At the San Diego Zoo, there's a sign near the rhinoceros enclosure that reads, "Stay back at least 20 feet and beware when I turn my back to you." The reason for the warning is that rhinos like to mark their territory with urine—and when you consider that the average male rhino weighs 4,500 pounds and is the second-largest land animal, you can imagine what happens when they do.

It's a funny thing about animals and their territory: They often make it a point to announce what belongs to them, and they exaggerate how much space they themselves actually occupy. Bears, for example, make scratches on

trees—not down low, but as high up as they can reach. Wild cats back up to rocks and trees and urinate upward. Dogs lift their legs and do the same thing.

"They're leaving their scent where other dogs will smell it, and they put it as high up as they can, so that it will appear that a big, macho dog has been there," says James H. Sokolowski, D.V.M., Ph.D., a veterinarian in Vernon, California. The best way for them to gain that extra height is to lift a leg, tilt their bodies slightly to the side, and aim for the highest spot.

Urine is loaded with pheromones, chemical scents that tell a lot about dogs—their sex, their social status, even what they eat. "It's amazing how much information dogs are able to gather from a scent," says Dr. Sokolowski. Every dog's urine has a different smell, so these scent markings are very personal signatures. They allow dogs to tell the world about themselves, and other dogs are very interested in learning more.

This dog is lifting his leg way above his hip so that he can make his mark as high as possible up the tree. Other dogs who find the scent will think he's bigger than he really is.

Dogs often investigate when another dog is lifting his leg. It's the canine equivalent of getting the news as soon as it's printed.

Aiming High, Aiming Low

Marking territory via leg lifting is mainly a guy thing, especially among dogs with big macho personalities, says Liz Palika, a trainer in Oceanside, California, and author of *Love on a Leash*. It doesn't matter how big they really are, she adds. They want to seem big. "I've seen a little beagle arch his back like a contortionist to get his urine up high," she says. "But I also know a 150-pound Newfoundland who never lifts his leg at all."

All of this leg lifting isn't as random as it appears. Dogs who share territory—in today's world, common territory may be the perimeter of a yard, a fire hydrant on a city street, or the trees in a public park—have developed an etiquette for who pees where. A boisterous, take-charge dog will always aim high. The quiet, more submissive dog who follows him is going to add his scent to the message board, but he doesn't want to appear arrogant or challenging. So he aims a little lower.

"If you take an intact male to the park, he might want to mark as many as 20 bushes and 15 light poles," Palika adds. "A neutered male would be more likely to hit only two or three places."

Female dogs also leave chemical scents when they urinate. Since they aren't as concerned as males with marking territory or making social displays, they usually squat rather than lift their legs. Some females, of course, have personalities that are every bit as outgoing and assertive as any male's, and these dogs sometimes lift their legs, Dr. Sokolowski says. So do females who have had medical problems that were treated with male hormones.

Not As Easy As It Looks

Just as it's a challenge for a person to stand on one foot, a dog has to learn to comfortably stand on three. It takes time for dogs to develop a good sense of balance, and puppies often struggle in the beginning. Dr. Sokolowski's dog, a Pekingese named Ming Tu, is a case in point. On his first attempt, he wound up flat on his back, spraying in the air.

"There are a lot of clumsy young males who fall while they're learning to pee with their legs up, but with practice they eventually learn to keep their balance," says Palika.

Dogs start working on their form when they're about 9 months old, and they keep practicing and perfecting it until they get it right. By the time they've reached a year and a half, the age of sexual maturity in most dogs, they're comfortable with the concept and are starting to think about refinements—such as marking higher in order to impress all the other dogs who will come after them.

Now That You Understand...

The urge to lift and water wouldn't be a problem if dogs only did it once or twice in the course of a walk. But dogs who are concerned about power and social status have an intense need to spread the word. This makes for some very slow walks—and worse. "Some dogs even mark inside people's homes," Palika says.

Since standing on three legs requires more concentration and balance than standing on four, you can take advantage of dogs' momentary distraction to teach them that they're not supposed to stop at every vertical object that they see. "When your dog lifts his leg, give the leash a tug," Palika says. "Tug just hard enough so that he has to put his leg down to catch his balance. When he does, give a command such as 'Don't pee.'" As long as you do this consistently, your dog will learn that he's only going to get a couple of chances to empty his bladder. He'll be more likely to do it all at once, rather than saving it up and releasing it a little at a time.

It doesn't take children very long to learn that there are appropriate times and places to urinate, and dogs can learn it too. The lesson "go potty" is among the easiest of all to teach, says Palika.

1. "Go outside with your dog when you know he has to go to the bathroom," Palika says. "The best time to practice is first thing in the morning, when you know he'll have to go."

2. As soon as your dog starts getting into position, tell him, "Go potty." He was going to do it anyway, so this step is easy.

3. As soon as he's done, give him a treat. Act as though it was all your idea and he's a great dog for listening and doing what he's told.

If you start this lesson when your dog is a puppy and you practice it every time he goes outside, he'll learn to control himself until you say that it's okay for him to go.

A slight tug sideways with the leash will pull dogs off balance and tell them that they don't have to sniff— or mark—every smell they come across.

CHAPTER FIFTY

TAIL WAGGING

Sending Messages, Revealing Moods

When you want to know what dogs are thinking, all you have to do is look at their tails. Tails are almost always in motion, and every motion means something different. "You can tell when a dog is feeling happy, aggressive, submissive, or worried just by looking at the wag of the tail," says Liz Palika, a trainer in Oceanside, California, and author of *Love on a Leash*. "Their tails always reflect their emotions."

The wag that we're most familiar with is the happy wag. Some dogs are so happy, in fact, that wagging their tails just isn't enough. They wag their entire back ends. "I love to see dogs with their rumps shaking," says Cynthia Jacobs, D.V.M., a veterinarian in Clarksville, Arkansas. "You know as soon as you see them that they are happy dogs and that they can't wait to meet you."

For all of this mobility and self-expression, tails aren't very sensitive, Dr. Jacobs adds. This is why dogs with big tails can walk through the house thumping furniture and knocking lamps off tabletops without noticing the destruction going on behind them. They don't even feel it.

Talking to You

Nature didn't give dogs expressive tails for the benefit of humans. They're really designed for long-distance communication with other dogs. Tails generally fly high above dogs' backs, allowing them to use them like flags to send messages from far away. They don't depend on this feature very much today, but it mattered a lot when dogs lived with other dogs. They could gauge the intentions and moods of strangers before they came within biting range.

Thousands of years of human interference have made tails less effective than they used to be. Greyhounds, for instance, have been bred so

The status of each dog is reflected in his tail. The big black dog signals dominance by holding his tail the highest. The other dogs are lower-ranking, so they hold their tails lower.

that their tails are perpetually held low or tucked between their legs. To other dogs, they look like they're always scared. Alaskan malamutes, on the other hand, have been bred to have their tails up all the time. They sometimes get into fights because they mistakenly convey the message that they're trying to be dominant.

Then there's the issue of docking. Airedales, cocker spaniels, and some other breeds have their tails docked, or cut short, when they're a few days old. This may look good in the show ring, but it leaves these dogs with a stubby appendage to do the job that their whole tails were meant to do. Dogs manage to adjust, but they probably lose a little bit of subtlety in their communications, says Dr. Jacobs. They appear to make it up in other ways—for example, by using their eyes or ears to convey messages that otherwise might be shown with the flick of a tail.

While all dogs use their tails in similar ways, there are some differences among breeds. Some hunting dogs, for example, have been bred to wag their tails constantly while going after prey. They only quit wagging when they've found what they're looking for. Herding dogs, on the other hand, have been bred to

A Tail of Recovery

When April got hit by a car, the prognosis was terrible. Her tail and both of her back legs were broken, and her veterinarian didn't think she'd walk again. "And she'll never wag her tail," he told Larry Anderson, April's owner and a Web site designer and computer programmer in Saint Cloud, Florida.

Against all odds, April proved him wrong. A month after the accident, she was able to stand. A month after that, she was walking. Soon after that, her tail started to wag—not as vigorously as before, but enough to show that she was coming back.

It's not much of a tail anymore, Larry admits. It's bulbous in the middle and a little on the crooked side. But it works, and it makes Larry happy every time he sees it. "When I come home, April moves it as fast as she ever did," he says.

American cocker spaniels usually have their tails docked, or cut short, in order to meet the standards of the American Kennel Club.

not move their tails very much, because vigorous wags could excite the animals that they're trying to herd.

Now That You Understand...

Experts in canine communication have identified many tail themes and variations. Here are the ones you'll see most often.

High and slowly swishing. Veterinarians hear it all the time: "I can't believe he bit me—his tail was wagging." People don't understand that wags aren't all the same and that there's a big difference between a happy wag and what experts call a swish. Dogs who raise their tails

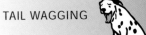

and slowly swish them back and forth aren't happy. "This usually happens when a dog is thinking dominant thoughts and is ready to back them up," Palika says.

Tail swishes are part of a whole communication package that includes puffing up the neck and moving the ears forward. Each of these things makes dogs look bigger and more ferocious. It warns other dogs or people to stay away.

Low and barely wagging. Just as dogs raise their tails when they're blustering, they lower them when they're intimidated. It's a sign of appeasement, a way of saying "Please don't hurt me—look how small and helpless I am."

Wagging madly. This is the wag that people like to see. Depending on the breed, the tail may be upright or pointing backward like a ruler. In

A thrashing tail could alarm these sheep, which is why herding dogs like this kelpie have been bred to keep their tails still while they're working.

either case, it will be beating the air wildly. This always signals a happy, enthusiastic dog.

TAXES AND TAILS

Until fairly recently, all dogs had long, expressive tails. Then, a few centuries ago, humans decided to make a few changes—not for the sake of the dogs, but, as often happens, to collect a little money.

The practice of docking, or cutting tails short, started in England. Dogs back then were divided into two groups—those who worked for a living, and those who were kept only for their owners' pleasure, explains Liz Palika, a trainer in Oceanside, California, and author of *Love on a Leash*. People who owned luxury dogs were required to pay a tax. Working dogs were tax-free. To collect taxes efficiently, officials needed to distinguish the workers from the loungers. So they came up with the idea of docking the working dogs' tails.

As the years went by and people got used to seeing certain breeds with truncated tails, this became a breed standard, an agreed-upon look that sets one breed apart from the rest. Many of the same breeds who get their tails docked today had working ancestors in the old country. Paradoxically, what began as a mark of common working dogs is now a sign of the canine elite—dogs who are deemed worthy to represent their breeds at the Westminster Kennel Club Dog Show and other prestigious dog shows.

CHAPTER FIFTY-ONE

THROWING UP

The Price of Opportunity

Dogs throw up so often and for so many reasons that veterinarians rarely bother trying to figure out what caused a particular episode. Essentially, they blame it on fate. "We call it GOK disease," says Robin Downing, D.V.M., a veterinarian in Windsor, Colorado. "It stands for God Only Knows."

Maybe it's because they get so much practice, but dogs don't seem to mind throwing up. Unless they're seriously ill with something, they aren't likely to lose much energy or even miss a meal. "Dogs have a much higher tolerance for physical discomfort than people," says Karen Campbell, D.V.M., a professor of small-animal medicine at the University of Illinois College of Veterinary Medicine at Urbana-Champaign. "Throwing up doesn't bother them nearly as much as us."

Feed the Mouth, Bill the Stomach

In order to understand dogs' facility for throwing up, it helps to understand how they view food in general. Their ancestors were hunters—but unlike most animals who hunt, they weren't very good at it. Dogs learned quickly that if they wanted to survive, they had to eat everything—fresh game, carrion, bones, even dirt and grass. And because their meals were sporadic, they got in the habit of really packing it in whenever they had the chance.

After eons of evolution, dogs have become totally nondiscriminating about food. They like everything. But not everything likes them back. "Dogs usually get upset stomachs because they've eaten spoiled food, too much food, or

Dogs will eat anything that smells—and anything that's sufficiently pungent has the potential to make them sick.

food that's too rich," says Dr. Campbell. They also tend to get sick when they eat rough things like bones or grass, which irritate the stomach.

Vomiting isn't good for carpets and wood floors, and it certainly isn't pleasant to witness or clean up. But it's fundamentally a healthy thing for dogs to do, says Tony Buffington, D.V.M., Ph.D., professor of clinical nutrition at the Ohio State University College of Veterinary Medicine in Columbus. "Dogs have much shorter intestinal tracts than people do, so they can clear the whole thing faster," he says. "Considering all the questionable things dogs eat, being able to get them out fast has a lot of survival value."

Can't Stomach Being Alone

We all know the feeling of stomach butterflies, which tend to swarm when we're nervous. Dogs get them too. There's a physical reason for this. Anxiety causes the stomach to produce more acid. The irritation, if it's strong enough, can stimulate stomach contractions that result in throwing up.

Probably the main source of stress for dogs is the one that's hardest to avoid: spending time alone. Nature never intended dogs to live apart from their canine—or, more recently, their human—families. Many dogs get anxious when they're alone, which can give them a queasy feeling. This is why people sometimes come home and find evidence that their dogs have been violently ill, even though the dogs seem to be perfectly healthy.

Small dogs tend to throw up more than bigger ones, Dr. Campbell adds. The reason is

Why do dogs always throw up on the carpets?

Put a dog in a large room with a vast expanse of easily cleaned tile. Should he need to throw up, he'll invariably wander off the tile and onto a carpet to lose his lunch. The more expensive the carpet, it seems, the better the odds that he'll hit it.

It's not entirely a coincidence. "Dogs have a strong instinct not to soil the spaces where they sleep, eat, and drink," says Myrna Milani, D.V.M., a veterinarian in Claremont, New Hampshire, and author of *DogSmart*. They're not really aiming for carpet, she adds. What they're doing is going as far as possible from their usual living area. And if that area happens to include an expensive Oriental rug, well, that doesn't bother them at all.

simple: They have little stomachs. Even a little bit of overindulgence can push them to the heaving point. The opposite happens too. Small stomachs may not hold enough food to last all day. The resulting hunger spasms can trigger bouts of vomiting, she explains.

Now That You Understand...

Give their bellies a break. Dogs with flu or other stomach viruses may keep getting sick as long as there's food in their stomachs, says Dr. Downing. She recommends putting them on a fast for a day. Going without food for 24 hours gives their stomachs a chance to recover, and they'll start feeling better fairly quickly.

Cook some rice and hamburger. A strange thing about dogs is that even when they've been throwing up, they'll often gobble their food just the same—then get sick some more. Dr. Downing recommends putting them on a rice-and-hamburger diet for a day or two. This combination is easy to digest and will help prevent a relapse, she explains.

Give them extra fluids. You don't want dogs to drink a lot of water when they've been throwing up, because that can stimulate more heaving. But it's important to replace the fluids that vomiting has removed from their bodies. Once the worst of the sickness is over, replace

CALL FOR HELP

Dogs throw up all the time, and usually it doesn't mean very much. You can get a good idea of how serious it's likely to be just by watching how they feel afterward. "If your dog throws up and doesn't look back, don't worry about it," says Robin Downing, D.V.M., a veterinarian in Windsor, Colorado. Dogs who are acting mopey, however, or who have vomited five or more times in 24 hours, need to see a veterinarian. Serious vomiting can be caused by poisoning, ulcers, or other internal problems. You should get help right away.

Dogs love human food, but it's frequently too rich for them to digest, which is why they may throw up afterwards.

your dog's usual water with Pedialyte, recommends Lynn Cox, D.V.M., a veterinarian in Olive Branch, Mississippi. Available in drugstores, this solution contains essential minerals called electrolytes. It will help prevent dehydration and keep dogs healthy. Pedialyte comes in several flavors. Most dogs prefer the orange, says Dr. Cox.

FAST FIX Some of the same over-the-counter medicines that people use also help pets who have been throwing up. When your dog has been sick, try giving him one chewable Pepto-Bismol tablet for every 25 pounds of weight. "They usually like the tablets better than liquids," says Dr. Cox.

If you don't have tablets, it's fine to give liquid Pepto-Bismol, Dr. Campbell adds. The usual dose is half of a tablespoon for every 15 pounds of dog, two or three times a day.

CHAPTER FIFTY-TWO

YAWNING AT THE VET'S

Instant Calm

There's a lot of yawning going on out there, and only some of it's at bedtime. Marathon runners yawn before races. Musicians yawn backstage before concerts. Brides yawn before weddings. And dogs yawn when they're waiting in the veterinarian's office.

Fatigue has little to do with all of these mouth-open, tongue-curling yawns. Research has shown that yawning causes instantaneous changes in the body, in dogs as well as in people. Heart rate goes up. Bloodflow to the brain increases. The lungs fill to capacity, taking in oxygen and whisking away carbon dioxide. All of these changes help dogs dispel anxiety, gather their wits, and focus on the tasks at hand, explains Ronald Baenninger, Ph.D., professor of psychology at Temple University in Philadelphia and a leading authority on yawning.

Few things in a dog's life are as exciting—and as nerve-racking—as waiting to see the veterinarian, adds Joanne Howl, D.V.M., a veterinarian in West River, Maryland. Even before they walk in the door, they're barraged with smells from unfamiliar (and sick) animals, strange people, and medications,

Even a routine visit to the veterinarian is a stressful experience. Yawning helps a dog to feel calmer and more focused.

antiseptics, and cleaners. Dogs can probably smell other dogs' fear as well as the nervousness of their owners, she says. It's not a reassuring environment, and it makes most dogs feel rather apprehensive. To calm themselves, they yawn—and keep yawning. "It helps them center themselves when they're really excited or agitated," Dr. Howl says.

Getting Pumped

Yawning helps dogs cope with all kinds of stress, not just stress that's caused by strange or frightening things, says Dr. Baenninger. Dogs who are

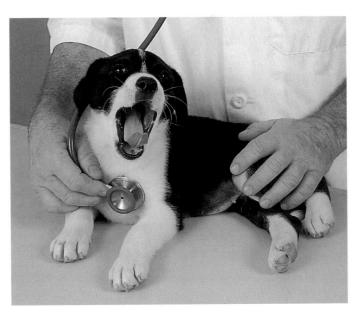

The water is making this Dalmatian nervous. Yawning releases tension from his body and floods his tissues with energizing oxygen.

anticipating something good will often yawn a few times to get their minds and bodies prepared. It gives them a surge of energy and helps control their eager agitation. "When I grab a leash, my dogs wake up fast, stretch, and give a big yawn. Then they're ready to go," he says.

Yawning was especially helpful back in the days when dogs had to catch their own suppers. Ancient dogs, just like dogs today, spent a lot of their time sleeping. It wouldn't do for them to be groggy after waking up, especially when a likely meal happened to wander by. They had to make the transition from dead-sleep to full alertness almost instantly, and yawning helped them do it.

All meat-eating animals use yawning as a kind of wake-up pill, Dr. Baenninger explains. Slower-moving, plant-eating animals—cows, for example—don't yawn very much. "They don't really have to get their energy up for much of anything," he says.

Mom Needs a Break

Puppies start learning about yawns within a few days of being born. Apart from doing their own yawning, they learn to watch their mothers' yawns. A yawn from Mom is a sign that it's time for the pups to settle down. Mother dogs probably don't use yawns as a deliberate form of communication, but when they're feeling comfortable and relaxed, their puppies naturally relax as well.

As adults, dogs will yawn to calm themselves in many situations. In training classes, for example, yawning can reach epidemic proportions. "You see it a lot in dogs who are really eager to please but don't know how," says Dr. Howl. Dogs who start getting frustrated will often yawn as a way of taking a mental break, she explains.

They do the same thing in veterinarian's offices. Some dogs will yawn nearly nonstop, especially when they're in the waiting room and aren't sure what's going to happen. Once an examination is underway, a yawn or two is a good sign, says Dr. Howl. "Sometimes I'll see a really tense dog on the table, and I'll start talking to her and petting her to settle her down," she says. "When she gives that big yawn, I know she's starting to come around."

Now That You Understand...

Yawn back. For dogs as well as people, the memory of Mom gives a lot of comfort. You can rekindle this soothing memory as a way of calming dogs when they're feeling anxious. The next time you're at the vet's, and your dog is looking nervous, give a big yawn of your own. Many dogs will respond the same way people do when someone yawns—by yawning back, says Dr. Baenninger.

It's best to start doing this when dogs are still young and are naturally attuned to watching for yawns, says Dr. Howl. If you start early, you can use this trick throughout their lives to keep them calm at the veterinarian's and in other stressful situations.

Take a break. A sleepy yawn now and then doesn't mean very much, but dogs who are giving one yawn after another are anxious about something. Yawning back isn't going to calm them down. What they really need is a break from the situation, says Dr. Howl. Rather than staying in the veterinarian's waiting room, for example, find out how much time there is until your appointment. If there's time, take your dog outside. A quick walk or even a big breath of fresh air will stimulate some of the same physical responses as yawning, she explains. Your dog will feel calmer and will be less upset when you come back inside.

People who train dogs always watch for yawns because they invariably mean their dogs have reached the end of their attention spans. They start yawning when they simply can't take in any more information. Pushing them at this point will increase their frustration and trigger even more yawning. Yawning means that it's time to do something else for a while, says Dr. Howl. Throw a ball. Run around for a few minutes. Give them a cookie. Even a short break will help them dispel nervous energy and shake the cobwebs from their brains.

PUPPY DOG TALES

How Kelsey Learned the Ropes

Kristen LaCroix of Aurora, Illinois, didn't plan to teach Kelsey, her 8-year-old beagle mix, to yawn on command—although she might have if she'd thought of it. As with all puppies, Kelsey was particularly adorable when she curled her little pink tongue and gave a big yawn. "Every time she yawned, she made a cute little sighing noise," Kristen says. "I would always look at her and say in a really stupid voice, 'Bi-i-ig yawn!'"

The message wasn't lost on Kelsey, who realized that yawning seemed to make her owner very happy. One night she had the opportunity to prove how alert she really was. Kristen and her husband, Pete, had guests over for dinner. Pete was telling them about Kristen's fascination with Kelsey's yawns. To demonstrate, he said, "Bi-i-ig yawn," imitating Kristen's voice. Kelsey, right on cue, ran to the table and gave a big, arching yawn.

After that, of course, Kristin couldn't resist telling Kelsey to yawn, and Kelsey is always happy to oblige.

Credits and Acknowledgments

(t=top, b=bottom, l=left, r=right, c=center, F=front, C=cover, B=back)
All photographs are copyright to the sources listed below.

PHOTOGRAPH CREDITS

Ad-Libitum: Stuart Bowey, i, viib, ixc, 2b, 3c, 4b, 5b, 6t, 7b, 9t, 10b, 11b, 12b, 14b, 15t, 16b, 17b, 18t, 19b, 20b, 25t, 26b, 28b, 29t, 30b, 32t, 34b, 35t, 36b, 38t, 39b, 41b, 42b, 44b, 46t, 48b, 49t, 50b, 51b, 52b, 53b, 55b, 56b, 57b, 63b, 65t, 67b, 70b, 71b, 73c, 74b, 76b, 84t, 85b, 87t, 88t, 89b, 91t, 92b, 94t, 95b, 97t, 98b, 99t, 101b, 102b, 105b, 106t, 107b, 108b, 110b, 112t, 115b, 116b, 121t, 122b, 124b, 125b, 126t, 127b, 129t, 134b, 136b, 137b, 138b, 138t, 139t, 140b, 141t, 142b, 144b, 144t, 146t, 147t, 150b, 152b, BCbl

Auscape International: Francais/Cogis, 133c, 156b; Gehlhar/Cogis, 13t; Hermeline/Cogis, 60b; Lanceau/Cogis, 23b, BClc

Australian Picture Library: 43b, 158t; Carnemolla, 153t

Bill Bachman and Associates: Bill Bachman, 22t, 59t

Norvia Behling: ivt, xb, 21t, 33b, 37b, 45b, 100, 104b, 113b, 128b, 148b, 157b, BCtl

Walter Chandoha: 149t

Bruce Coleman Limited: Adriano Bacchella, 131t; Erwin and Peggy Bower, 80b; Jane Burton, 8b, 82c, 120b; Jorg and Petra Wegner, 119b, BCtr

Kent and Donna Dannen: 109t

Matt Gavin-Wear: 86b, 75t

Robert Harding Picture Library: 83b

The Image Bank: Frank Whitney, 27t

Ron Kimball Photography: Ron Kimball, xii, 132

NHPA: 31b

The Photo Library: 61t

PinchMe Design: Jacqueline Richards, 54b, 151b

Dale C. Spartas: 40, 66, 145b, 154b

Renee Stockdale: 64b

Stock Photos: ii

Tony Stone Images: John Brown, FC

Judith E. Strom: viiit, 62t, 68b, 118b, 130b, BCrc

The publisher would like to thank the following people for their assistance in the preparation of this book:
Peta Gorman; Sally Gorman; Tracey Jackson; Aliza Pinczewski; The Royal Society for the Prevention of Cruelty to Animals, Yagoona, N.S.W., Australia; Danielle Wilkes

Special thanks to the following people who kindly allowed their dogs to be photographed:
Steve Allen and "Ren"; Len Antcliff and "Bozie"; Aruna Basmayake and "Nikki" and "Maggie"; Tara Beath and "Jax"; Corinne and Don Braye and "Minne"; Sue and Michelle Burk and "Jacko"; Pam Cohn and "Jesse"; Lynn Cole and "Abel" and "Suzie"; Lindy Coote and "Boo"; Adrian Cox and "Polly"; Donna and Tom Devitt and "Kinka"; Frances Farac and "Madison"; Annette Fitzgerald and "Bundy"; Bev Flowers and "Jack"; Kevan and Verena Gardner and "Floyd"; Gwynneth Grant and "Max"; Roger Goldsinch and "Buzz"; Kerri Hancock and "Marley"; Lindy Haynes and "Babar"; Richard Hennassey and "Beau"; Philip Jacobs and "Casper," "Rogue," and "Tinker"; Emilia Kahrimanis and "Lulabel"; Sherrie Martin and "Max" and "Sam"; Paul McGreevy and "Wally"; Andrew McIntyre and "Abby" and "Daisy"; Louise Moore and "KC" and "Zammy"; Judith Neilson and "Pepa"; Karl Pitt and "Bengie"; Simmone Pogorzelski and Shaun Lawrence and "Jackson"; Jacqueline Richards and Nick Wiles and "Skipper"; Jennifer Saunders and "Barney" and "Kitty"; Ann and Richard Stevens and "Cassie"; Alex Syriatowicz and "Socrates" and "Cassiel"; Cassandra and Jason Toogood and "Saba"; Amanda Trickey and "Rusty"; Sarah-Jane Vaux and "Dessa"; Russ Weakley and Anna Gregg and "Max," "Bob," and "Harry"; Annabella Zanetti and "Frank"

Index

Boldface page references indicate photographs. <u>Underscored</u> references indicate boxed text.